The Letter to the Hebrews

OneBook.

DAILY-WEEKLY

The Letter to the Hebrews

Ken Schenck

Cover design by Strange Last Name
Page design by PerfecType, Nashville, Tennessee

Schenck, Kenneth, 1966-
   The Letter to the Hebrews / Ken Schenck. – Frankin, Tennessee : Seedbed Publishing, ©2018.

   pages ; cm. + 1 videodisc – (OneBook. Daily-weekly)

   An eight-week Bible study.
   ISBN 9781628245202 (paperback)
   ISBN 9781628245240 (DVD)
   ISBN 9781628245219 (Mobi)
   ISBN 9781628245226 (ePub)
   ISBN 9781628245233 (uPDF)

   1. Bible. Hebrews -- Textbooks. 2. Bible. Hebrews -- Study and teaching. 3. Bible. Hebrews -- Commentaries.   I. Title. II. Series.

BS2775.55.S33 2018   227/.8706   2018932515

 Seedbed

SEEDBED PUBLISHING
Franklin, Tennessee
seedbed.com

CONTENTS

Week Four

Trust in the Priest 38

Week Five

Don't Fall Away 50

Week Six

The Perfect Sanctuary and Sacrifice 62

WELCOME TO ONEBOOK DAILY-WEEKLY

John Wesley, in a letter to one of his leaders, penned the following:

> O begin! Fix some part of every day for private exercises. You may acquire the taste which you have not: what is tedious at first, will afterwards be pleasant. Whether you like it or not, read and pray daily. It is for your life; there is no other way; else you will be a trifler all your days. . . . Do justice to your own soul; give it time and means to grow. Do not starve yourself any longer. Take up your cross and be a Christian altogether.

Rarely are our lives most shaped by our biggest ambitions and highest aspirations. Rather, our lives are most shaped, for better or for worse, by those small things we do every single day.

At Seedbed, our biggest ambition and highest aspiration is to resource the followers of Jesus to become lovers and doers of the Word of God every single day, to become people of One Book.

To that end, we have created the OneBook Daily-Weekly. First, it's important to understand what this is not: warm, fuzzy, sentimental devotions. If you engage the Daily-Weekly for any length of time, you will learn the Word of God. You will grow profoundly in your love for God, and you will become a passionate lover of people.

How Does the Daily-Weekly Work?

Daily. As the name implies, every day invites a short but substantive engagement with the Bible. Five days a week you will read a passage of Scripture followed by a short segment of teaching and closing with a question for reflection and self-examination. On the sixth day, you will review and reflect on the previous five days.

Weekly. Each week, on the seventh day, find a way to gather with at least one other person doing the study. Pursue the weekly guidance for gathering. Share learning, insight, encouragement, and most importantly, how the Holy Spirit is working in your lives.

That's it. Depending on the length of the study, when the eight or twelve weeks are done, we will be ready with the next study. On an ongoing basis we will release new editions of the Daily-Weekly. Over time, those who pursue this course of learning will develop a rich library of Bible learning resources for the long haul.

OneBook Daily-Weekly will develop eight- and twelve-week studies that cover the entire Old and New Testaments. Seedbed will publish new studies regularly so that an ongoing supply of group lessons will be available. All titles will remain accessible, which means they can be used in any order that fits your needs or the needs of your group.

If you are looking for a substantive study to learn Scripture through a steadfast method, look no further.

INTRODUCTION

The letter to the Hebrews has two main points. It has a main teaching point; namely, that the offering of Jesus on the cross has forever taken care of our sins. No other sacrifice is required. We need no priest but Christ to reconcile us to God. Atonement is accomplished. By God's grace, salvation is ready and available for us to sign up for at any time.

The other main point is the implication of atonement. The audience needs to continue in faithfulness. They have no reason to doubt the truth of the message they have heard. They must not give up. They have every reason to cross the finish line and, indeed, the consequences would be dire if they do not.

We do not know many other aspects of Hebrews for certain, but these basic truths are clear enough. These two points hold true no matter what the specifics of the audience's situation. Did Hebrews warn its audience not to rely on the temple? Or did Hebrews console them after the temple was already destroyed? Either way, the point is that we need no further means of atonement. Jesus is all we need. Was the audience tempted to fall back into Judaism? Or was a group of Gentile believers having second thoughts about the God of Israel? Either way, the message to endure remains.

Hebrews 1:1–12

Celebrating Jesus

INTRODUCTION

The book of Hebrews is in many ways one of the most puzzling books in the New Testament. We do not know who wrote it, and we are unsure of the church to which it was written. Experts on the book disagree on when it was written and whether its recipients were primarily Jewish or non-Jewish. Many think that its first twelve chapters were meant to be read as a sermon to a congregation the author hoped to visit in the near future.

The first chapter begins majestically, with an almost hymn-like contrast of Christ with the angels. Next to God himself, surely angels are the most exalted of God's creations. Yet next to Christ, they are nothing. They are only servants in the kingdom of the universe. To show the glory of the age that Christ is inaugurating, Hebrews 1 shows us how much more glorious Jesus is than the angels, the stewards of the age that is now passing away.

ONE

A Definitive Word

Hebrews 1:1–2 NRSV *Long ago God spoke to our ancestors in many and various ways by the prophets, ²but in these last days he has spoken to us by a Son, whom he appointed heir of all things, through whom he also created the worlds.*

Key Observation. From the very moment God started to create to the moment that Christ will bring his eternal kingdom, Jesus is God's last Word for the universe.

Understanding the Word. The first two verses of Hebrews present a contrast. In the past, God spoke to his people in many different ways. He spoke to his people through human prophets in Israel. He spoke to them through angels. He led them through the wilderness with a pillar of fire and a wandering cloud.

In days recent to the author, God had inaugurated a new Word: Jesus. He is not just one of many but *the* one Word. This final Word was the Son of God, the King to restore the rule of God on earth as it is in heaven. For centuries Israel had been without a king. They had hoped for God to give them full control of their land back.

In Jesus, they received a King greater than they could have possibly imagined. They received a people that was much bigger than those who had Jewish blood. They became part of a kingdom that was not only bigger than the land of Israel, not only bigger than the Roman Empire, but a kingdom that consisted of the whole universe, of all things both seen and unseen. The previous ways that God had spoken were "many and various." Now God had spoken a singular, final Word in Jesus.

Jesus the Son spans the whole of history. On the one hand, he is the "heir of all things." Everything that exists in the creation will be his when the kingdom fully comes. God has bequeathed it to him as his Son. In 1 Corinthians 15:26–27, we learn that God has destined everything in this world to be put under Christ's feet, including death. So when Hebrews says that Jesus is the heir of everything, it truly means that Christ will rule over everything that God has made.

Then we learn that Jesus was actually at the beginning of the creation as well. This Son who is heir of everything was also the One through whom God created the worlds. Christians have long taken this statement to mean that Jesus must have existed before he came to earth as Christ. In fact, we believe that Jesus is God. In some mysterious way, even though there is only one God, God exists as three persons—Father, Son, and Holy Spirit.

Hebrews 1:2 tells us that Christ was the agent of creation. Some Jewish writings from the time of the New Testament speak of God creating the world by means of his wisdom. An Old Testament example of this way of thinking is Proverbs 8:22–31, where God's wisdom is pictured at his side helping him create the world. Might the author of Hebrews have been hinting to this congregation that Jesus was God's wisdom for the world, the One who gives meaning to everything? Jesus is the Word God spoke to heal the world.

So begins this majestic sermon. Jesus is at the beginning and end of history. Jesus is God's last Word for the universe. We know that we are about to hear God's answer to all the world's questions and problems. We are about to know the secret to the universe from the beginning to the end of time. That answer and that secret is Jesus Christ.

1. Have you ever pondered the awesomeness of Christ? How great is this One who spans time from eternity past to eternity future! Are you living with an awe proper to his greatness?

2. How different would your community of faith look if Jesus were truly King? What is God calling you to do to make any needed changes?

3. Since Jesus is, in fact, God's wisdom for the universe, should we not share that wisdom with as many people as we can? Are you excited to let God's wisdom speak to everyone and every part of your own life?

TWO
The Image of God

Hebrews 1:3–4 *The Son is the radiance of God's glory and the exact representation of his being, sustaining all things by his powerful word. After he had provided purification for sins, he sat down at the right hand of the Majesty in heaven. ⁴So he became as much superior to the angels as the name he has inherited is superior to theirs.*

Key Observation. If you want to know what God is like, look at Jesus. Jesus is a perfect reflection of who God is and the One who will make the universe what it is supposed to be again.

Understanding the Word. There are some books that we do not consider Scripture today that were nevertheless of great value to the earliest Christians. The author of Hebrews seems to draw on one of them in verse 3. The "Book of Wisdom" said something very similar to this verse when it was talking about

God's wisdom. In this book, God's wisdom is said to be the radiance of God's eternal light and an image of his goodness.

The author's point seems to be that if you want to know how wise God is, look at Jesus. Do you want to know what God is like? Look at Jesus. If you want to understand God's plan for the world, pay attention to Jesus. In Jesus, we find a mirror of God the Father. God is glorious. He is so full of glory that we would not be able to look at him if he appeared to us. Jesus radiates and reflects that glory.

In some way, Jesus sustains all things. As Colossians 1:17 says, he holds everything together. Sin has put the whole universe off-line. It is not working as it should. In Jesus, God is hitting the Reset button on the world. Everything will work right once Jesus' salvation is fully in place. He is the solution to hold together everything that is falling apart.

Jesus is the glue that can reattach us to God. All have sinned and are lacking the glory of God (Rom. 3:23). We are separated from God. But Jesus is the One who can reconcile us to our Father and Creator.

This work is done, although it is not yet fully enacted. Jesus' death has paid for the work. He has taken a seat because the purification is accomplished. God, the greatest Majesty there is, has enthroned him and installed him as King of the cosmos. Christ became lower than the angels for a little while (Heb. 2:7), but now that the work is done, God has exalted him far above any angel. He is now enthroned far above all principalities and powers (e.g., Col. 1:16).

What is the name he has inherited? The next verse will prompt us to think Hebrews is talking about the name of a son. While we often think of a name in terms of a person's name, it probably refers to Jesus receiving the *title* of "Son of God." Tomorrow we will explore what this title "Son" probably means in Hebrews.

What we see clearly in this rich collection of statements about Christ is how exalted he truly is. He shows us who God is. He shows us the very essence of what the universe is meant to be about. He has, in one faithful act, forever reconciled us to God. He made a purification for the sins of the world and then sat down because the work was done. We now only await his return for everything to be finally restored.

The angels are still helping us, but their role as ministers of the creation is coming to an end. Before long, the King who is not seen will be seen, and every knee will bow before Jesus Christ our Lord.

1. Although Jesus uniquely reflects God's glory in some respects, are we good reflections of who God is to those around us? When others look at us, do they see Jesus?

2. Are we glue, not only in our churches, but in our communities? Do people tend to hold together when we are around, or are we a dividing force? What changes do we need to make?

3. Jesus has set in motion the restoration of all things. Are we spreading the word? Are we participating in his mission of reconciliation?

THREE

Jesus Is King

Hebrews 1:5–6 ESV *For to which of the angels did God ever say, "You are my Son, today I have begotten you"? Or again, "I will be to him a father, and he shall be to me a son"?*

⁶And again, when he brings the firstborn into the world, he says, "Let all God's angels worship him."

Key Observation. "What a friend we have in Jesus!" Yes, but he is also our Lord and Master. Every knee must eventually bow and every tongue confess that Jesus, the King, is Lord.

Understanding the Word. Although we naturally think of sonship in terms of biological offspring, the background to this term in many parts of the Bible has to do with kings. In parts of the Old Testament, we can see that when a king was installed, he was thought in a sense to become God's son. The first two verses that Hebrews quotes in 1:5–6 both referred originally to human kings.

The first quote comes from Psalm 2, which was an enthronement psalm. It is suggested that this psalm might have been read at the coronation of kings. "Today"—on the day of enthronement—God declared that the king was being installed as God's "son." The second quote from 2 Samuel 7:14 clearly refers to David's son Solomon. While David was in prayer, God told him that Solomon, David's biological son, would be God's son as king, and God would be a father to Solomon.

As Christians, we believe, of course, that Jesus has been the Son of God for all eternity past. One of the early creeds of Christianity clarifies that Jesus was "eternally begotten of the Father, begotten, not made." One of the most famous debates in the 300s was whether Jesus was the first thing that God created when he made the universe or whether Jesus had always existed. The church strongly concluded that Jesus has *always* existed as God's Son.

Nevertheless, although Jesus was the heir apparent to the throne for all eternity, the New Testament gives us the sense that he was officially installed as King after his resurrection and exaltation to God's right hand. Jesus came to earth, lived out the human experience, and died to atone for the sins of humanity. Then the One who was always destined to rule the universe finally took office!

Experts debate exactly when the angels worshipped Jesus in 1:6. Because we know Jesus' birth story in Luke 2 so well, it is tempting to think Hebrews is thinking of the "angels we have heard on high, sweetly singing o'er the plain." It is possible; it is also possible that the author of Hebrews had the second coming in mind. Hebrews seems to be quoting a version of Deuteronomy 32:43, which has a strong sense of God's judgment.

However, in the flow of Hebrews 1, it is more likely that Hebrews 1:6 is talking about the angels worshipping Jesus when he entered into heaven after finishing atonement, rising from the dead, and returning to heaven. As Jesus returned to the throne room, the angels bowed before him who was also their King, enthroned officially over them as well as humanity and the rest of the creation. The world Hebrews has in mind is the coming world spoken of in 2:5.

If the angels bow before King Jesus, how much more should we? How easy it is in our time to think of Jesus as our buddy and God as our daddy! Yes, we are immensely privileged to call God our Father and Jesus our Brother. But Jesus is also our King, and we are also part of God's kingdom. Jesus is our Lord, our Master, in addition to being our friend.

1. Where are you on the spectrum between Jesus being your buddy and Jesus being your King? Do you have a healthy balance between communion and awe?

2. Does the community of faith to which you belong bow before their King? When is the last worship service when you sensed the awesomeness of Christ?

3. Are you an ambassador of King Jesus to the community and world around you? Are you bringing fairness, redemption, and mercy to your world?

FOUR

The Divine King

Hebrews 1:8–9 NRSV *But of the Son he says, "Your throne, O God, is forever and ever, and the righteous scepter is the scepter of your kingdom. ⁹You have loved righteousness and hated wickedness; therefore God, your God, has anointed you with the oil of gladness beyond your companions."*

Key Observation. Jesus is both fully human and fully divine. As God, he rules over all the creation. As a human, he showed us true righteousness.

Understanding the Word. Hebrews 1 has a series of contrasts between Jesus and angels. We do not know exactly why. Some have speculated that the audience may have thought of Jesus as more of an angel than the Son of God. Others wonder if this church had too high a view of angels. What we do know is that angels were the primary ministers of the old covenant (1:14), and since Jesus had started a new covenant, the angels would soon no longer need to watch over humanity.

Verse 7 points out how angels are like winds and flames of fire. They are also servants. The Greek being translated makes it clear that we are to see this verse in contrast with the verses that follow.

For example, while the angels are servants, the verses for today indicate that Jesus is not only King, but he is God. He is the One we all must serve, alongside the angels. Similarly, the roles the angels play are temporary. They come, play their role, then go away. By contrast, Jesus' royal role as King will never end. His throne is forever and ever.

Hebrews 1:9 points out a key characteristic of Jesus as King: he is righteous; he rejects wickedness. The human Jesus faced choices when he was on earth, just as we do. In each case, Jesus chose righteousness. Therefore, as the book of Acts says repeatedly, God raised him from the dead. God anointed him with an "oil of gladness." This is an allusion to the coronation ceremony of a king, where the new king is anointed.

We will see in the second chapter that humanity, men and women, are Jesus' brothers and sisters. It is from among these companions that Jesus has been anointed King. He is both like us and yet unlike us. He is like us in that he has partaken of the same flesh and blood that we have (2:14). He is like us in that he was tempted and tested just as we are (4:15). He is the pioneer of our faith (3:1; 12:2) who wants to lead us to the same glory he has attained (2:10).

He is also quite different from us. He is God. He is the King. As King, Jesus will now reign with a righteous scepter. He is our King and the King of the universe.

As Christians have reflected on these verses, they have seen a glimpse of the divinity of Jesus, just as we also see a glimpse of his humanity. We believe as Christians that Jesus is and was both fully human and fully divine. As God, he is our King. As human, he is our Brother.

We have the blessing to have inherited centuries of godly Christians reflecting on passages like these. Jesus is the last Word for creation, but it took several centuries to unpack that significance. This unpacking most definitively took place in the New Testament, but the unpacking continued in the first few centuries. What a privilege it is for us not to have to figure all these things out from scratch. The Holy Spirit has already given us not only the Bible but also some common understandings of it.

1. Do you think of Christ as an example of righteousness to follow? How would you live differently if you did?

2. Are the leaders of your community known for their righteousness? If you are such a leader, are you someone who leads with righteousness?

3. When you see injustice, are you and your community part of the solution?

FIVE

The Forever King

Hebrews 1:10–12 *He also says, "In the beginning, Lord, you laid the foundations of the earth, and the heavens are the work of your hands. [11] They will perish, but you remain; they will all wear out like a garment. [12] You will roll them up like a robe; like a garment they will be changed. But you remain the same, and your years will never end."*

Key Observation. This world will soon pass away, but Jesus will be King for all eternity. He was here at the beginning of time and he will be here long beyond its end.

Understanding the Word. These three verses are the second part of a contrast between Christ and the angels that began in 1:7. Angels may be like winds and flames in their temporary service for humanity, but the years of Christ as King will never end. In fact, the whole of the current creation will eventually wear out and perish. It is not merely the winds and flames that come and go. The current role of angels as servants to the created realm will eventually pass. By contrast, Christ's rule and his role is permanent.

As in 1:2, these verses suggest that Christ in some way served as the agent of creation, as the instrument through which God made the world. Significantly, Hebrews here quotes a verse that in the original psalm was about Yahweh, about God the Father (Ps. 102:25–27). It is thus natural that we hear in these verses some of the most exalted language about Jesus in the New Testament. These verses reinforce the Christian sense that Jesus is fully God, of one substance with God the Father even though he is a distinct person.

Jesus remains the same. He remains the same not only in his role as King but in his character and desire to help us. One of the themes we will see later in Hebrews is the fact that in Jesus there is help for us on the journey. What a relief to know that Jesus will never change his love for us! As the final chapter of Hebrews says, Jesus is the same yesterday, today, and forever (13:8). The same Jesus who was there for the early church is also available as our intercessor as well.

Another theme we will see near the end of Hebrews is the fact that the current creation will, at the very least, be transformed when Christ returns. This world is currently enslaved to some of the same forces of decay and corruption that we are (cf. Rom. 8:19–21). Nevertheless, this age is passing away and will soon come to an end, in God's timing. Then God will change the clothes of this earth like taking off a coat.

Several passages in the Bible talk about both the judgment and the new creation. Second Peter 3 talks about the destruction of the current world by fire. Hebrews 12:26 talks about how God will remove the skies and the earth that are part of God's current creation. But this is not the end of the story in Scripture. Revelation 22 speaks of new skies and a new earth. It speaks of a heavenly Jerusalem that will come down to earth. Then all it seems that will be left for the angels to do is to worship God (Heb. 12:22).

This current world is going to pass away. Of course, that is not an excuse for us to forget about what God wants to do here and now. It seems hard for us to keep from going to extremes. A person can be "so heavenly minded that they are no earthly good." Probably most of us are too this-worldly minded, meaning that we live for now and do not take enough stock in the fact that this world is temporary and about to pass away. These verses remind us about the truly temporary nature of this world.

1. Do you tend to focus more on the world that is to come or on the problems of today? How might you reorient your focus in whichever way is most needed?

2. Things that we do for others, we do for Christ. They are eternal deeds. How is our community of faith doing in regard to the deeds of eternity?

3. Even though the creation is decaying, God has given it to us to steward. How is your community doing as stewards of God's world?

WEEK ONE

GATHERING DISCUSSION OUTLINE

A. Open session in prayer.

B. View video for this week's readings.

C. What general impressions and thoughts do you have after considering the video and reading the daily writings on these Scriptures? How have you grown deeper in your faith and understanding of Scripture?

D. Discuss questions selected from the daily readings.

    1. **KEY OBSERVATION:** From the very moment God started to create to the moment that Christ will bring his eternal kingdom, Jesus is God's last Word for the universe.

    DISCUSSION QUESTION: How different would your community of faith look if Jesus were truly King? What is God calling you to do to make any needed changes?

    2. **KEY OBSERVATION:** If you want to know what God is like, look at Jesus. Jesus is a perfect reflection of who God is and the One who will make the universe what it is supposed to be again.

    DISCUSSION QUESTION: Although Jesus uniquely reflects God's glory in some respects, are we good reflections of who God is to those around us? When others look at us, do they see Jesus?

3. **KEY OBSERVATION:** "What a friend we have in Jesus!" Yes, but he is also our Lord and Master. Every knee must eventually bow and every tongue confess that Jesus, the King, is Lord.

   DISCUSSION QUESTION: Are you an ambassador of King Jesus to the community and world around you? Are you bringing fairness, redemption, and mercy to your world?

4. **KEY OBSERVATION:** Jesus is both fully human and fully divine. As God, he rules over all the creation. As a human, he showed us true righteousness.

   DISCUSSION QUESTION: Are the leaders of your community known for their righteousness? If you are such a leader, are you someone who leads with righteousness?

5. **KEY OBSERVATION:** This world will soon pass away, but Jesus will be King for all eternity. He was here at the beginning of time and he will be here long beyond its end.

   DISCUSSION QUESTION: Even though the creation is decaying, God has given it to us to steward. How is your community doing as stewards of God's world?

E. Close session with prayer.

WEEK TWO

Hebrews 2:1–18

The Story of Salvation

INTRODUCTION

In some ways, the first and second chapter of Hebrews go together. Together, they tell us where we are in the story of salvation. Hebrews 1 celebrates that Jesus has been enthroned as King of the universe, far above the angels. Hebrews 2 gives us further backstory.

You see, we humans were supposed to be the glorious rulers of the world. Unfortunately, it has not played out that way because of our sin. So Jesus became human. Jesus became lower than the angels for a little while. Because he was without sin, he was able to defeat the devil. Now he is our High Priest who wants to lead us to the glory we were supposed to have in the first place.

ONE

The First Warning

Hebrews 2:1–3 *We must pay the most careful attention, therefore, to what we have heard, so that we do not drift away. ²For since the message spoken through angels was binding, and every violation and disobedience received its just punishment, ³how shall we escape if we ignore so great a salvation? This salvation, which was first announced by the Lord, was confirmed to us by those who heard him.*

Key Observation. We often think of the vastness of God's grace, but equally staggering to contemplate are the consequences of drifting away from him.

13

Understanding the Word. Today's verses are the first of several interruptions the author makes to the train of thought in order to make clear to the audience of Hebrews what is at stake. The author regularly interrupts his teaching in order to do some preaching. Each time he interrupts, he warns the audience about the consequences of not continuing in faith. By these warnings, he urges them to keep going in faith until they finally make it to the end.

Hebrews 2:1–3 is the first of these interruptions, the first of these warnings. It follows closely on Hebrews 1, where the author has shown in exalted terms that Jesus is greater than the angels. Now he comes to the implication. If Jesus is more exalted than the angels, as Hebrews 1 says, then the word he has delivered is an even more serious matter than any word that the angels might have delivered.

Hebrews 2:2 passes on the Jewish tradition that the Law of Moses was delivered to Moses by way of angels. The "message" about which it speaks is the Pentateuch, the first five books of the Bible. These laws were binding on Israel. When someone in Israel disobeyed them, they were punished, at times quite harshly. For example, a number of violations of the Jewish Law were punishable by death, such as if a person committed adultery.

This Law delivered by angels was very weighty. We can read about some of the consequences of disobeying this "message spoken through angels." Hebrews 12:20 mentions that any animal had to be stoned that even accidentally touched the mountain where the Law was delivered.

If the first covenant was that serious, then the new covenant inaugurated by Jesus must be even more serious, since Jesus is greater than the angels. This way of thinking may be foreign to some of us, but Hebrews is probably suggesting that the punishment for abandoning Christ will be much more severe than the punishment for violating the Law of Moses.

This is a major theme of Hebrews. The audience cannot turn back from Jesus because the consequences are extremely dire. They cannot let themselves "drift away." They need to pay attention. They need to continue in faith. They will not escape if they do not. The judgment is coming, and salvation is only possible through Christ.

God also has given them every reason to believe that this coming salvation is real. He verified it with the miracles that Jesus did while he was on earth (2:4). This is a theme we find in Acts 2 as well. The signs and wonders that followed Jesus and the early apostles were proofs from the Holy Spirit that Jesus and these individuals were, indeed, from God.

On a side note, Hebrews 2:3 is one of the strongest hints that the apostle Paul was not the author of Hebrews. In his letters, Paul makes it very clear that he is a direct witness to Jesus (e.g., 1 Cor. 9:1). It would be unusual for Paul to put himself in the second tier of those in contact with Jesus.

1. Hebrews 2:1–3 can be jarring to a culture that has largely lost a sense of the seriousness of abandoning God. How do these verses make you feel? What is your immediate reaction?

2. What would our communities of faith look like if we took these verses seriously? How would they change?

3. How would the urgency of our mission to the world around us change if we took the message of these verses seriously?

TWO

Created with Honor

Hebrews 2:5–8 NRSV *Now God did not subject the coming world, about which we are speaking, to angels. ⁶But someone has testified somewhere, "What are human beings that you are mindful of them, or mortals, that you care for them? ⁷You have made them for a little while lower than the angels; you have crowned them with glory and honor, ⁸subjecting all things under their feet." Now in subjecting all things to them, God left nothing outside their control. As it is, we do not yet see everything in subjection to them.*

Key Observation. It is amazing that God cares and watches over us, even though we seem so small in the light of the whole universe!

Understanding the Word. The next few verses of Hebrews 2 set up a kind of drama. The plot begins with God intending for humans to rule over the creation. As we will find out in later verses, this intention is not yet fulfilled. But the psalm the author quotes, Psalm 8, at least shows us God's ideal and original intention.

Even though we are just mortal human beings, God cares for us. God is "mindful" of us. He made us lower than the angels, at least for a little while. When God created the world in Genesis 1, he created humanity in his image, both male and female (Gen. 1:27). As God rules over the creation, humanity was intended to have the whole creation "under their feet."

What an amazing insight into our value as humans. We cannot treat any life lightly because every human being is a tiny reflection of God. Every human being was intended for honor. As the poet John Donne wrote in, "No Man Is an Island," "Any man's death diminishes me, because I am involved with mankind" (Meditation XVII). To mess with another human being is to mess with God.

God, of course, did not intend for us to abuse the creation with this authority. If God is love, then his rule over the creation is not an abusive one but a caring one. So also, if humanity should stand in a position of honor within the creation, we would need to take the same mindfulness and care for the creation, for this is the job that God first gave us. We should be good stewards of that which God has entrusted to us.

It is indeed puzzling that anyone would think it appropriate to exploit God's world. There are some that think God would not allow us to inflict any permanent harm on this world. Yet God regularly allows us the freedom to do wrong and to hurt others. If God allows human beings to murder other human beings, we should assume he would let us inflict permanent damage on our world.

We thus should assume responsibility for our actions and do everything in our power to be good stewards of God's world. If we use his creation, let us work to replenish it as well. Let each generation leave it at least as good as we received it, and hopefully leave it even better.

It is amazing to think that God has this much care for us. The more we have discovered about the universe, the smaller we seem in the vast scheme of things. We are but a tiny speck on a tiny planet in an obscure solar system in just one of countless galaxies in a vast universe. Yet the God who created this vast domain is mindful of us. Indeed, he is mindful even of the tiniest sparrow (see Matthew 10:29; Luke 12:6).

These verses seem to say that humanity will, indeed, rule in the coming age as God had originally intended for this current one. Angels minister to us now, but we will not need them to minister to us then. A day is coming when humanity will play their intended role, and all that will be left for the angels is to worship God and bow before King Jesus (12:22)!

1. Are you able to receive this tremendous love God has for you? Spend some moments to take in the staggering truth that the God of the universe cares for *you*.

2. Are we as mindful of each other in the church as God is for us? If God can take time for us, why can't we take time to care for each other?

3. Are we mindful of those outside our church walls as God is for them? What are we going to do to be more like our heavenly Father?

THREE
We Have a Problem

Hebrews 2:8–10 ESV *Now in putting everything in subjection to him, he left nothing outside his control. At present, we do not yet see everything in subjection to him. ⁹But we see him who for a little while was made lower than the angels, namely Jesus, crowned with glory and honor because of the suffering of death, so that by the grace of God he might taste death for everyone.*

¹⁰For it was fitting that he, for whom and by whom all things exist, in bringing many sons [and daughters] to glory, should make the founder of their salvation perfect through suffering.

Key Observation. Jesus solved the human problem by living without sin and then dying for us so that we might rule with him forever.

Understanding the Word. Now we see the problem. God created humanity to be the glorious leaders of the earth. We are to rule as good stewards and protectors of the world. By contrast, not only are we not in control of the world but we have lost control of ourselves. Because of Adam's sin, we find ourselves slaves to the power of sin. We all in the course of our lives sin many times like Adam. All have sinned and are lacking the glory of God that he intended us to have as in Psalm 8 (Rom. 3:23).

We do often exercise power over the world, but it is not as good stewards or good rulers. We deface God's earth without giving it a chance to replenish itself. We exploit the world's resources. We often take little thought for the effect of our God-given expansion of knowledge on the world or those around us. When we have the power, we often use it to our own advantage in a way that hurts or oppresses others. Instead of being good kings, we tend to be tyrants who need to be deposed.

"But we [do] see [Jesus]" (v. 9). Jesus troubleshoots the human problem by entering into humanity. The way this verse is worded in the Greek builds suspense until Jesus is revealed as the solution to the human problem. Humanity did not fulfill its role. But we see someone who was made lower than the angels. We see this person crowned with glory and honor. We see Jesus! He is the first to fulfill this psalm, but he will not be the last.

For a little while, he is made lower than the angels too. Unlike humanity, because he was without sin, he was worthy of the glory and honor that God intended for us all. He suffered death for everyone. We all die because we are in Adam. But those who come to be in Christ will not die but will live forever. Jesus came so that he might lead many sons and daughters to their intended glory.

Jesus was perfected through his sufferings, not because he was imperfect before or had some moral deficiency, but because he would not be ready to provide atonement until after he had completed his appointed task in death. The word *perfect* in Greek had a sense of completion. Jesus was not complete to serve as a priest until he died on the cross and rose from the dead.

After he finished his sufferings, he is now perfect to take away our sins. He is now ready to serve as our High Priest. He is locked and loaded as someone who can provide atonement.

Jesus is thus the first person under whom God has put the coming world. But he will not be the last. We will reign with him. On the one hand, let there be no doubt that he is, in fact, our King. But at the same time, we will reign together with Christ for all eternity in fulfillment of God's perfect plan.

1. Are you willing to follow the path of Jesus to eternal glory? It is often a path of suffering. It is a path that leads away from sin.

2. Do you enter into the problems of others? Do you rejoice with those who rejoice, and mourn with those who mourn?

3. Jesus tasted death for anyone who would rely on him. Are you willing to deny yourself for those around you for whom you can be a servant?

FOUR

Defeating Death

Hebrews 2:14–15 NRSV *Since, therefore, the children share flesh and blood, he himself likewise shared the same things, so that through death he might destroy the one who has the power of death, that is, the devil, [15]and free those who all their lives were held in slavery by the fear of death.*

Key Observation. God made the One who was without sin to become sin for us "so that in him we might become the righteousness of God" (2 Cor. 5:21 NRSV).

Understanding the Word. John 1 not only tells us that Jesus existed before he came to earth, and it not only tells us that Jesus is God. John 1:14 tells us that "the Word became flesh and lived among us, and we have seen his glory, the glory as of a father's only son, full of grace and truth" (NRSV). John 1:1 is one of the key passages in the Bible telling us that the virgin birth was not the beginning of Jesus' life. He existed from eternity past as God, long before he finally stepped into human flesh.

Hebrews 2:14 tells us something similar. God the Son wanted to save humanity from the predicament they found themselves in—intended for glory but lacking it. So Jesus also became human, just as God planned before the world was created. He became a human so that he could solve the human problem. He took on blood and flesh.

Flesh and blood are not evil in themselves. Otherwise, Jesus would not have taken them on. A few decades after Hebrews, a group called the Gnostics would arise, a group that believed matter and flesh were evil. The Gospel of John perhaps was written in part with a view to their false teaching.

So the problem with flesh is not that it is intrinsically evil. But for Paul and the author of Hebrews, blood and flesh have become a tool of Satan's power. Even when the spirit is willing, the flesh—unless we have the Holy Spirit with us—is weak in the face of temptation. Our flesh became enslaved to the power of sin after the time of Adam. Without the Spirit, it remains enslaved today.

Humanity received a death sentence as a result of Adam's sin. The devil, this verse says, now has the power of death, and there is nothing *we* can do about it. But there was something that Jesus could do about it. He could beat the devil at his own game. He could partake of flesh and blood but break the power of sin over flesh.

This feat is exactly what Jesus did and now he wants to break the power of death over us for all eternity. He also wants to break the power of sin over our lives even today. In the words of the hymn, "O for a Thousand Tongues to Sing": "He breaks the power of cancelled sin; he sets the sinner free. His blood can make the vilest clean. His blood availed for me."

We need not fear death. Death is not the end for us. Death is only the beginning of eternity, an eternity in which we will reign with Christ.

Nor need we be slaves to the power of sin. The power of the Spirit can give us the strength to face temptation with confidence, and the power of Jesus' resurrection will one day give life to our mortal bodies.

Romans 7 and 8 present the possibility of freedom from sin. In Romans 7:14–25, Paul presents the plight of someone who actually wants to do the right thing but simply cannot do it in their own power. The good they want to do is not done. Many stop their reading of Romans there.

But Romans 8 goes on to speak of the victory that is possible in this area through the power of the Spirit. "Those who are in the realm of the flesh cannot please God" (Rom. 8:8). But the Spirit can set us "free from the law of sin and death" (8:2).

1. Do you ever struggle with a certain temptation? Do you tend to think of defeat as inevitable? What would it look like to trust in the power of God more?

2. Fear is contagious. But the love of God for us should help us overcome fear. How can your community of faith move toward hope in the face of God's power rather than fear?

3. If we really believed that Jesus conquered death, would it change how openly we spread the good news to others? Would we not want everyone to know?

FIVE

We Have Help

Hebrews 2:16–18 *For surely it is not angels he helps, but Abraham's descendants.* ¹⁷*For this reason he had to be made like them, fully human in every way, in order that he might become a merciful and faithful high priest in service to God, and that he might make atonement for the sins of the people.* ¹⁸*Because he himself suffered when he was tempted, he is able to help those who are being tempted.*

Key Observation. Jesus is willing and able to come to our assistance when we are struggling with the temptation to run away from suffering.

Understanding the Word. Some experts on Hebrews think that 2:17–18 are the key verses of the whole sermon. These verses are the first time when the sermon mentions that Jesus is our High Priest, which is the major teaching of Hebrews. Jesus is our go-between with God, the One who has made it possible for us to be reconciled to him. We can keep going if we just keep our eyes on him.

The author reminds us of Hebrews 1 when he says that Jesus did not come to help angels but to help humanity. In particular, Jesus came to help "Abraham's descendants." The author of Hebrews does not mean that Jesus only came to help those who are Jewish. Hebrews almost certainly means everyone who confesses Jesus as their King, both Jew and non-Jew. Those of us who have faith become children of Abraham, and those who do not have faith are not truly the children of Abraham.

Some have wondered if the audience only thought of Jesus as an angel or an angel-like figure. That might explain why Hebrews emphasizes that Jesus came to help humans—and thus took on their blood and flesh—rather than angels. Perhaps they thought Jesus had become an angel after his death. It is hard to know for sure what they were thinking. These sorts of suggestions are just guesses that no one could ever prove.

What Hebrews 1 does make very clear is that Jesus did not come to earth as an angel. Nor is he an angel now. He came to earth as a human being and he ascended to heaven as a human being who is much greater than the angels. The coming world will be ruled by Christ and humanity, not angels. We do not know the full story of why Hebrews takes so much time to make this contrast, but we know Jesus' identity for sure.

The bottom line for the audience is that Jesus is ready and willing to help if they begin to struggle, especially if they begin to doubt or wonder if everything they have heard is true. Jesus is a merciful High Priest who wants to forgive and come to their aid. Jesus is a faithful High Priest, whom they can always count on to be available. He has been tempted. He has suffered while being faithful. He knows what they are going through. He can help in their time of need.

The high priesthood of Jesus is the central teaching of Hebrews. The author will devote chapter 5 as well as chapters 7 through 10 to this subject. The audience does not need to worry about having any other means of atonement because Jesus has taken care of everything. Accordingly, they can and must continue walking in faithfulness.

Should they doubt, Jesus will not be unsympathetic. He, too, faced suffering. He faced the cross. He was tempted to run away, to take the easy way out. But he moved forward in obedience and faithfulness, just as they must.

1. Do you ever find yourself trying to go it alone? Would you live life differently if you truly relied on Jesus as your High Priest?

2. Does your community of faith ever try to go it alone without depending on God? Would your church move forward differently if you collectively relied on Jesus as your High Priest?

3. Even though humanity has become enslaved to sin, humanness must not be automatically sinful because Jesus became human. Can you see the value of humanity as a whole the way that Jesus did?

WEEK TWO

GATHERING DISCUSSION OUTLINE

A. Open session in prayer.

B. View video for this week's readings.

C. What general impressions and thoughts do you have after considering the video and reading the daily writings on these Scriptures? How have you grown deeper in your faith and understanding of Scripture?

D. Discuss questions selected from the daily readings.

    1. **KEY OBSERVATION:** We often think of the vastness of God's grace, but equally staggering to contemplate are the consequences of drifting away from him.

    DISCUSSION QUESTION: Hebrews 2:1–3 can be jarring to a culture that has largely lost a sense of the seriousness of abandoning God. How do these verses make you feel? What is your immediate reaction?

    2. **KEY OBSERVATION:** It is amazing that God cares and watches over us, even though we seem so small in the light of the whole universe!

    DISCUSSION QUESTION: Are you able to receive this tremendous love God has for you? Spend some moments to take in the staggering truth that the God of the universe cares for *you.*

    3. **KEY OBSERVATION:** Jesus solved the human problem by living without sin and then dying for us so that we might rule with him forever.

DISCUSSION QUESTION: Do you enter into the problems of others? Do you rejoice with those who rejoice, and mourn with those who mourn?

4. **KEY OBSERVATION:** God made the One who was without sin to become sin for us "so that in him we might become the righteousness of God" (2 Cor. 5:21 NRSV).

   DISCUSSION QUESTION: If we really believed that Jesus conquered death, would it change how openly we spread the good news to others? Would we not want everyone to know?

5. **KEY OBSERVATION:** Jesus is willing and able to come to our assistance when we are struggling with the temptation to run away from suffering.

   DISCUSSION QUESTION: Do you ever find yourself trying to go it alone? Would you live life differently if you truly relied on Jesus as your High Priest?

E. Close session with prayer.

WEEK THREE

Hebrews 3:4–19; 4:9–13

Entering God's Rest

INTRODUCTION

Hebrews 1 builds on the fact that Christ is greater than the angels. The angels were those who mediated the first covenant that God gave to Moses. Hebrews 3 now makes a second comparison between Jesus and the old covenant. Jesus is greater than Moses. Moses is even more associated with the old covenant, with the Jewish law, than the angels were. Moses was one of the greatest Israelites of all time, the great lawgiver, the great mediator of Scripture. Yet Jesus Christ is greater still. Moses was a servant in the household of God. Jesus is the Son par excellence.

The preacher of Hebrews does not spend long on this contrast, however. He quickly moves once again to urge the audience to continue in faith. Moses led the people of Israel out of Egypt. They had a promise of a special homeland. They headed toward a promised land. Yet almost none of them made it because of unbelief and a lack of faith. The author uses this illustration to give the audience a stern warning. You have left Egypt with Jesus. Be sure to be faithful until you make it to the heavenly city.

ONE

God's Household

Hebrews 3:4–6 *For every house is built by someone, but God is the builder of everything. ⁵"Moses was faithful as a servant in all God's house," bearing witness to what would be spoken by God in the future. ⁶But Christ is faithful as the Son* *over God's house. And we are his house, if indeed we hold firmly to our confidence and the hope in which we glory.*

Key Observation. We are sons and daughters in God's household, brothers and sisters of the Son of the house, Jesus.

Understanding the Word. The main argument of Hebrews begins in chapter 3. The author has introduced the main theme of Hebrews at the end of Hebrews 2: the fact that Jesus is our High Priest. Hebrews 3 then begins to consider what it might mean to understand Jesus as a High Priest.

The first stop on this journey is a comparison between Jesus and Moses. We saw in Hebrews 2 that the Law was delivered through angels (2:2). Those angels in turn delivered it *to* Moses. Moses was the most important figure in Jewish history. It was to Moses that God revealed the agreement of the first covenant at Mount Sinai.

At the time of Christ, most Jews thought of Moses as the author of the Pentateuch. It was through Moses that God delivered Israel from the bondage of slavery in Egypt. It was to Moses that God gave instructions to build the sanctuary in the wilderness, and it was Moses who met with God so closely that God's glory shined on his face.

But Jesus was inaugurating a new covenant, and a better one at that! The author wanted to make it clear that Jesus is on a much higher level than even Moses. Moses gave witness to Jesus as the One who was coming. But Jesus is the One Moses anticipated. Jesus is the One who is greater than Moses.

Both were, of course, faithful to God. But Moses was faithful as a servant in God's household. By contrast, Jesus was a Son. Like the angels, Moses was a servant, but Jesus is the King himself. Moses must bow down to Jesus as the angels bowed down before Jesus.

There are two images of a house in these verses that blur into each other. The first is that of a physical house. The author of Hebrews reminds them that God is the One who builds every house, including the house of God's people. Nothing that exists came to be without God's planning and construction.

Then Hebrews shifts to *house* as household. Within the household of God's people, Moses is only a servant. Jesus inherits the house. Jesus will own the house. Moses only serves in the house.

In that same household, we are brothers and sisters of Christ (2:12). As Jesus is a Son, so are we also sons and daughters in God's household. However, as in Hebrews 2:1–4, the author does put a condition on it. Hebrews 2:1–4 says that since Christ is greater than the angels, and those who disobeyed the word delivered through them, then those who abandon Christ face an even more serious consequence. So Hebrews 3 will go on to make that argument with regard to Moses.

We are in God's household "if indeed" we hold fast in our boldness and in our boasting about the hope we have in Christ (3:6). On the other hand, if we abandon him, we have no basis to think we are still in his house. If we no longer consider him our King and rebel against his kingship, then we become enemies of his house. The "if indeed" was a sober warning to the audience to stay in the household!

1. The warnings of Hebrews are nothing to fear for those who love Christ, no matter how we might fail. Have you ever considered how serious a matter it would be to abandon him?

2. Hebrews is addressed to a whole community. Can a community abandon Christ? If so, what might that look like?

3. Have you ever thought about evangelism as a matter of inviting others into your family? How might that impact the way you approach those who do not believe?

T W O

Every Day Is Today

Hebrews 3:12–14 NRSV *Take care, brothers and sisters, that none of you may have an evil, unbelieving heart that turns away from the living God. [13]But exhort one another every day, as long as it is called "today," so that none of you may be hardened by the deceitfulness of sin. [14]For we have become partners of Christ, if only we hold our first confidence firm to the end.*

Key Observation. Every day is a "today" when we need to reaffirm our faith in Christ and enter into the promised land.

Understanding the Word. The first six verses of Hebrews 3 talk about how Christ is greater than Moses, just as he is greater than the angels. At that point, as he has done before and will do again, the author interrupts his train of thought with a warning. If those who did not believe what God had to say through Moses did not make it to the promised land, then how much more serious will be the consequences for those who do not persist to the end with Jesus!

In Hebrews 3:7–11, the author quotes Psalm 95:7b–11. Hebrews has the longest quotations of the whole New Testament, and it is clear that the author believed these passages from the Old Testament to be inspired. He introduces the quote by saying that these words are the words of the Holy Spirit.

When the Holy Spirit speaks through Scripture, it becomes more than just what God was saying from one author to one audience. When the Holy Spirit speaks, the words take on a living quality that moves beyond the place and time when God originated them. So the psalm in this case is not just a warning to Israel from the time of the psalmist, but it is a warning to the audience of Hebrews and it is a warning to us today.

In the quote, God is talking about how the generation that left Egypt did not make it to the promised land. They did not make it because they hardened their hearts in the desert. They rebelled against their God. So God determined that they would not enter into the rest of the promised land.

A hardened heart is a dying heart. A hardened heart cannot pump blood to the body. A hardened heart cannot have faith, and without faith it is impossible to please him (Heb. 11:6).

When we come to the verses for today, the author draws the appropriate conclusion. The audience also needs to be careful that they do not develop an unbelieving heart like the wilderness generation. They should not be hardened by the deceitfulness of sin like the generation in the desert. What kind of sin does the author have in mind? A sin of disbelief in the promises of God. They are doubting and perhaps on the verge of abandoning their faith in who Jesus is and in the God of Israel.

Every day, the author suggests, is a day to decide to enter the promised land. Every day called today is a day for faith. "Today," Psalm 95 reaches across the centuries and says, "do not harden your hearts" (vv. 7b–8a). Today, we choose by God's grace and power to enter again into the promised land. Have you chosen God today?

Hebrews uses a special Greek tense in 3:14. We became partakers of Christ at some point in the past, and we remain partakers now in the present if we are holding fast in our affirmation of him. The tense speaks to some action that is not only completed, but an action that has remained completed from then till now. The implication is that if we stop moving forward through life with faith, our participation in Christ cannot and will not continue.

1. Have you entered into the promised land today?

2. Are you an encouragement to others toward faith and confidence in Christ as we journey together through the wilderness of our lives?

3. Doubt is not yet turning away. In fact, there is often great faith behind honest doubt. But it is best not to doubt alone. Who are the people who strengthen your faith? Is there anyone who might undermine it? Resolve to spend most of your time with those who strengthen it.

THREE
Don't Stop in the Desert

Hebrews 3:15–17, 19 ESV *As it is said, "Today, if you hear his voice, do not harden your hearts as in the rebellion." ¹⁶For who were those who heard and yet rebelled? Was it not all those who left Egypt led by Moses? ¹⁷And with whom was he provoked for forty years? Was it not with those who sinned, whose bodies fell in the wilderness? . . . ¹⁹So we see that they were unable to enter because of unbelief.*

Key Observation. The promised land is real and straight ahead. Do not waver in your trust that there is a land of promise around the corner but keep going forward!

Understanding the Word. The analogy between Israel's decision and the decision of the audience is made very clear here. Israel had left Egypt. They were on their way to the promised land. It was the journey of a lifetime, one that involved trials and the testing of their faith.

The audience believed in Christ. In the words of Hebrews 6:4, they already shared in the Holy Spirit. According to Hebrews 10:26, they already appropriated the sacrifice of Christ. They were on the journey of a lifetime, and they were facing trials.

We should not think that "partaking" is something short of becoming a Christian. Some have attempted to say that they have only dabbled in faith, not truly embraced it. But this is only an expression. Hebrews 2:14 says that Jesus "partook" (ESV) of flesh and blood, and 2:9 says that he "taste[d]" death. Yet it is overwhelmingly clear that Jesus really and fully died, and he truly and fully became human.

The problem with the Israelites in the desert is that despite how good a start they had leaving Egypt, their corpses fell in the desert. They did not make it to the promised land. They grumbled and doubted and, in the end, did not reach the goal. Hebrews gives us no sense that they will be part of the coming kingdom of God. Their failure was a final failure.

The implication for the audience is again crystal clear. If they do not continue and endure in their faith, they will not enter into the kingdom of God. They will not be part of the rest that is yet to come. If they do not continue in faith, they will not reach the goal. If they turn away from faith, it will be a final failure.

The sin that Hebrews has in mind, as we will see later on, is not just any sin. It is a sin of apostasy. It is a sin of abandoning Christ and deciding not to confess him as King any longer. It is turning away from the living God. Experts on Hebrews disagree on whether the audience was primarily Jewish or non-Jewish. If the audience was Jewish, then these were Jews who are wondering whether Jesus truly was the Messiah. If the audience was non-Jewish, then they were unclear whether the living God of Israel was, in fact, the supreme God after all. They might be tempted to go back to their dead idols and the gods of Rome.

Throughout Hebrews, the author will argue that God has made promises, just as God made promises to Israel when they left Egypt. He promised that Jesus would return to become King of the world. God promised that an unshakeable kingdom would come and that they would be part of it. Were they going to continue believing these promises or were they going to be like the wilderness generation, who did not believe that God was powerful enough to conquer the land of Canaan?

The bottom line is to believe! The message is to keep on slogging through the desert, even though we may have to face times of testing and trial. Do not turn away from the God who is truly alive. It will be worth it in the end!

1. Can you imagine being so close to Christ himself in time and yet being tempted to turn away? On the other hand, if the audience of Hebrews could keep going, surely we can as well!

2. Although most of the spies doubted whether Israel could take the land, there were two who had faith. Are you resolved to be one of those who believes in God's promises?

3. Have you ever considered what effect wavering in faithfulness might have on those who do not yet believe? How might your resolve for faith increase if you considered the potential effect of your life on those around you?

FOUR

Rest Ahead

Hebrews 4:9–11 *There remains, then, a Sabbath-rest for the people of God; ¹⁰for anyone who enters God's rest also rests from their works, just as God did from his. ¹¹Let us, therefore, make every effort to enter that rest, so that no one will perish by following their example of disobedience.*

Key Observation. Scripture calls God a "God of peace" several times in the New Testament. We have every reason to be at rest when we are trusting in God!

Understanding the Word. The train of thought at the beginning of Hebrews 4 can be difficult to follow at some points. The reason is that the author of Hebrews is using an old Jewish method of arguing from Scripture. In Psalm 95, God talks about how he did not allow the Israelites in the desert to enter into the promised land, which the psalm calls God's "rest." So Hebrews asks, What is God's rest?

This is the point where Jewish methods of interpretation came into play. The Holy Spirit led the author's mind to Genesis 2:2, where God *rests* after creating the world. What does it mean to finally enter God's rest? The author's mind was taken to the point of creation when God rested. Surely we will find out there, the author thought, what "the rest of God" is.

When God rested, he moved beyond his creation activity. Hebrews indicates that for us to enter into God's rest we must move beyond the age of this creation into the new creation. Although the passage is not entirely clear, the author is possibly referring to our final rest, after we have moved beyond this world to the next.

The author uses an intricate argument to suggest that the promise of entering God's rest did not end when Joshua finally led Israel into Canaan (4:8). Psalm 95 speaks of Israel not entering into God's rest and it was written long after Joshua. Thus the author concludes that the promise of rest still remains open for the audience and for us. The rest could not have happened when historical Israel entered the promised land because the psalmist was still waiting for that entrance much later.

A wise scholar once concluded that God's rest is both something we must enter into today and yet something that we will not enter into until God finally restores the world. Every day that is "today," we must choose to enter God's rest. Yet we will not finally enter into God's Sabbath rest until we are done with this creation and its work. Similarly, we must hold fast until our final day on this earth if we hope to remain partakers of Christ.

When I woke up this morning, did I make the choice to enter God's rest? "Lord, I choose to enter your rest today and for today to be a day of faith." Only if I continue to enter God's rest every day will I once and for all enter it at the time of God's final kingdom.

There are other truths you might see in this passage, even if they were not likely what the author of Hebrews had in mind. For example, although he probably was not thinking this way, we know from Paul that we become right with God by trusting in him, not by trying to earn our salvation. We are made right by faith, not works.

Similarly, Christians who have not fully surrendered themselves to God will no doubt find a war within between their flesh and the Spirit. Some have seen in this passage a hope for rest from the conflict between the part of us that is given to God and parts of ourselves that we may want to hold on to. Only if we let go entirely can we find rest from this inner war.

1. Are you at rest with God because you have placed your trust in him not only for today, but for eternity as well?

2. Are you at rest within because you have surrendered everything to God and are, therefore, no longer in turmoil between temptation and following God's Spirit?

3. Are you at peace in the world, regardless of your circumstances, because you know that God is in control and will prevail in the end?

FIVE

The Word of God

Hebrews 4:12–13 NRSV *Indeed, the word of God is living and active, sharper than any two-edged sword, piercing until it divides soul from spirit, joints from marrow; it is able to judge the thoughts and intentions of the heart. [13]And before him no creature is hidden, but all are naked and laid bare to the eyes of the one to whom we must render an account.*

Key Observation. Our lives are an open book to God, who sees and knows everything. What other option is there but to follow him in our hearts as well as with our lips?

Understanding the Word. It is common to think of the Bible when you read the "word of God." So many Christians think of the Bible when they read Hebrews 4:12. Certainly that is true. God has spoken and continues to speak through Scripture in a way that exposes our hidden thoughts. God can use the Bible to lay our souls bare before him.

Similarly, some might think that these verses had Jesus in mind, since John 1 refers to Jesus repeatedly as the Word of God. Jesus is God's last Word for us and his universe. The final reconciliation of the world to God is a result of this Word. Jesus is God's will in action, and God has spoken Jesus for our salvation.

Yet these verses do not explicitly mention Jesus. In the end, the author of Hebrews probably had a much broader sense of God's word in view. Because we do not live at the time Hebrews was written, we would not know anything about this background if someone did not tell us.

There is a history in both Judaism and Greek philosophy behind the phrase, "the word of God." One group of Greek philosophers called the Stoics believed that the word of God controlled everything that happened in the world. It was God's will for the world, against which was useless to fight. Some Christians think of God's will very much in this way. "Everything happens for a reason," they might say.

Around the time of Christ, some Jews took this Stoic idea and applied it to Genesis 1, where God speaks and the world is created. God says, "Let there be light," and there is light. God's word became a way of talking about God putting his will into effect, God making things happen.

Therefore, when Hebrews talks about the word of God, it seems to be talking about God's will in action. God speaks, and it happens. And this verse especially seems to have in mind God's will when it comes to judgment. God speaks and we are judged.

We mentioned the Book of Wisdom when we were looking at Hebrews 1:3. There is an interesting parallel in it where God's word takes a sword and judges the Egyptians. In the Book of Wisdom, the destroying angel on the night of the Passover is likened to God's word in action, doing what God wanted it to do.

These verses in Hebrews tell us that there is nothing we do or intend that God does not thoroughly know. The whole creation is "laid bare" before him. He can distinguish our thoughts and intentions. He can discern between things that cannot be separated like soul and spirit or joints and marrow. There is no hiding from him.

This fact should be a great relief to us if we are truly his followers. There is no pretense with God. There are no secrets to hide. He knows it all. If we are in relationship with him, it should assure us that the One who wants to protect us knows what is really going on.

Therefore, we can be completely open with him. We can rest from the effort of defending a lie with another lie. Our lives are an open book with him. How foolish it would then be to do anything but follow him completely!

1. Does it bother you or reassure you that God knows your heart completely? Is there anything in your heart that you would not want him to see?

2. Do people in church ever play games with each other because they cannot see each other's intentions? What would the church be like if we were as transparent with each other as we are to God?

3. How honest are we with those in our communities outside the church? Do they trust our motives or have we given them reason to doubt our integrity? What would the world think if it could see our thoughts and intentions?

WEEK THREE

GATHERING DISCUSSION OUTLINE

A. Open session in prayer.

B. View video for this week's readings.

C. What general impressions and thoughts do you have after considering the video and reading the daily writings on these Scriptures? How have you grown deeper in your faith and understanding of Scripture?

D. Discuss questions selected from the daily readings.

    1. **KEY OBSERVATION:** We are sons and daughters in God's household, brothers and sisters of the Son of the house, Jesus.

    DISCUSSION QUESTION: Have you ever thought about evangelism as a matter of inviting others into your family? How might that impact the way you approach those who do not believe?

    2. **KEY OBSERVATION:** Every day is a "today" when we need to reaffirm our faith in Christ and enter into the promised land.

    DISCUSSION QUESTION: Have you entered into the promised land today?

    3. **KEY OBSERVATION:** The promised land is real and straight ahead. Do not waver in your trust that there is a land of promise around the corner but keep going forward!

    DISCUSSION QUESTION: Although most of the spies doubted whether Israel could take the land, there were two who had faith. Are you resolved to be one of those who believes in God's promises?

4. **KEY OBSERVATION:** Scripture calls God a "God of peace" several times in the New Testament. We have every reason to be at rest when we are trusting in God!

   DISCUSSION QUESTION: Are you at rest with God because you have placed your trust in him not only for today, but for eternity as well?

5. **KEY OBSERVATION:** Our lives are an open book to God, who sees and knows everything. What other option is there but to follow him in our hearts as well as with our lips?

   DISCUSSION QUESTION: How honest are we with those in our communities outside the church? Do they trust our motives or have we given them reason to doubt our integrity? What would the world think if it could see our thoughts and intentions?

E. Close session with prayer.

WEEK FOUR

Hebrews 4:14–16; 5:1–14

Trust in the Priest

INTRODUCTION

The thread of the discussion in Hebrews about Jesus as a High Priest continues at Hebrews 4:14. The author told us he was going to begin teaching on this subject back when he began chapter 3. But he did not get far before he was back to preaching about the church's need to keep pressing forward with faith.

Now he returns by reminding the audience that they have a merciful High Priest who wants to come to their aid. The strong warnings of Hebrews might be discouraging if it were not for the fact that God is on our side to get us through. True, there was a generation of Israel that fell in the desert and never made it to the promised land. But it did not have to be that way for them. Hebrews 5 will begin to describe for them this great priest they have on their side.

ONE

Approach God's Throne

Hebrews 4:14–16 NRSV *Since, then, we have a great high priest who has passed through the heavens, Jesus, the Son of God, let us hold fast to our confession.* *[15]For we do not have a high priest who is unable to sympathize with our weaknesses, but we have one who in every respect has been tested as we are, yet without sin.* *[16]Let us therefore approach the throne of grace with boldness, so that we may receive mercy and find grace to help in time of need.*

Key Observation. In Jesus we have a helper who both knows our needs and eagerly wants to come to our aid when we need it.

Understanding the Word. These verses closely parallel 10:19–25. In that way, they serve as a kind of opening parenthesis for these middle chapters of the book of Hebrews, a parenthesis that is then closed in chapter 10. The parentheses say that these chapters from 4–10 all go together. All these chapters are about Jesus as our High Priest.

In 4:14–16, the author summarizes the key takeaway from the fact that Jesus is our High Priest. We have every reason to keep believing. We have every reason to keep confessing that Jesus is our King. We can count on him to take care of our sins. He is a High Priest on whom we can depend.

First, Jesus has passed through the heavens. This fact alludes to a theme Hebrews will develop in later chapters. The earthly sanctuary and temple of Judaism was never the real temple of God. The real temple of God is the sanctuary of heaven, where God's throne is.

Some think there is an actual structure in heaven. I personally suspect that the author was thinking of heaven itself as the true sanctuary. In either case, to say Jesus passed through the heavens is to say that he has performed his atoning work in the true sanctuary rather than the imitation that was down here on earth.

Second, we have a sympathetic High Priest. Jesus is not bothered by our pleas for help. Perhaps you have been unfortunate to be dependent on someone who did not really want to help you. Perhaps your situation forced you to go to them, but you dreaded it because you knew they had no interest in giving you what you needed.

Jesus is nothing like that. Not only is he able to help us, but he wants to help us. He is sympathetic to our problems. He even sympathizes with our weaknesses. We should have no hesitation to go to him for help if we really and truly want his help, because he will give it.

This last point is perhaps the most surprising. Jesus has been tested like us. Other translations say he has been tempted like us. We often do not think of the human side of Jesus. We tend to think of him only in his divinity and ignore his humanity. But these verses tell us that Jesus knows what it is like to be tempted not to do the right thing.

The church to which Hebrews was sent was struggling with endurance in the face of difficulty. They may have feared an approaching persecution. They may have had worries about whether their sins could be forgiven if they did not rely on the temple.

Jesus also was tempted not to go through with suffering. In the garden of Gethsemane he prayed for the cup of suffering to pass from him if possible. But he did not shrink back from the next step. He endured. He continued forward in faith.

Jesus knows something about the temptation to turn away. Not only did he endure, but he wants to help us get through as well. We can approach God's throne with boldness and find the strength we need to face trials and temptations.

1. Have you ever been at the mercy of someone who did not really like you? How reassuring is it to know that the very person who *can* help us *wants* to help us with his whole heart?

2. Sometimes we do not really want help. We may want to solve our problems on our own. Are you willing to rely on Christ rather than on yourself?

3. Do you model being available to give grace to help to others in their time of need? Should we not be like Jesus to the world?

TWO

Priests Intercede

Hebrews 5:1–3 *Every high priest is selected from among the people and is appointed to represent the people in matters related to God, to offer gifts and sacrifices for sins. ²He is able to deal gently with those who are ignorant and are going astray, since he himself is subject to weakness. ³This is why he has to offer sacrifices for his own sins, as well as for the sins of the people.*

Key Observation. The purpose of a priest is to intercede for people to God. Jesus is the only priest we need.

Understanding the Word. The high priestly thread of Hebrews started with the key verses in 2:17–18. It briefly started at the beginning of chapter 3 with a contrast between Jesus and Moses. Then yesterday's verses resumed it with a direct encouragement to the congregation to rely on this Jesus who has passed through the heavens into God the Father's very presence.

Chapter 5 now steps back and asks what the characteristics of a priest are in the first place. First of all, you cannot simply decide to become a priest. It is a matter of appointment, and only those who are from the right lineage can be priests. Under the old covenant, you had to be a descendent of Levi, one of the twelve sons of Jacob. Later on in Hebrews 7, the author will argue that Jesus stands in the most important line of priests of all—the priestly order of Melchizedek. These are priests who do not come from a human family line.

Priests represent the people. They are chosen to represent the people to God and God to the people. They are both one of the people and yet they are in a special category. So also Jesus was fully human. Although he was God, he was chosen from among humanity to represent humanity as their priest. His qualification, we will find out in Hebrews 7, is that he has an indestructible life.

The specific way in which priests represent the people to God is by offering gifts and sacrifices for sins. It is not easy for us who did not grow up offering blood sacrifices to get a good sense of what people in Bible times were thinking when they offered so many sacrifices. Sacrifice may have been such a fundamental way of life for them that they themselves might not have been able to say.

Today, we often think of sacrifice as satisfying a need for justice or punishment, but it probably went much deeper in biblical times. Leviticus 17:11 told Israel that the life was in the blood. So it may not have been so much the death of the animal that brought atonement, but the life that was in the blood that came from the animal. What a different way of looking at sacrifice! It becomes the unleashing of the power of life rather than primarily being the punishment of death.

Earthly priests understood their need for reconciliation with God. They knew their sins. They knew their need. They not only needed to offer sacrifices for the people, but they had to offer sacrifices for themselves as well. Hebrews will argue that this fact made them inferior as priests to the One who did not need to offer an atonement for himself—Jesus.

Part of the message of Hebrews is that, with Jesus having offered the final sacrifice, we need not worry about having any more priests. The deed is done. The last priest is still on the job. We can find help at any time. This fact does not mean that ministers are not helpful today or that we should abandon all our relationships. God uses them to be sure. But we do not need any of them to get right with God.

1. Do you think of Jesus as someone you can go to and rely on or as so far away that he is not relevant to your life?

2. Although Jesus is our only priest, do you offer prayers for the other people in your church, family, and social circles?

3. Does your church offer gifts and sacrifices to God for your community and the world?

THREE

Jesus Appointed

Hebrews 5:4–6 ESV *And no one takes this honor for himself, but only when called by God, just as Aaron was.*

⁵So also Christ did not exalt himself to be made a high priest, but was appointed by him who said to him, "You are my Son, today I have begotten you"; ⁶as he says also in another place, "You are a priest forever, after the order of Melchizedek."

Key Observation. Jesus is the only King and priest we will ever need. He remains them forever, and he is perfect at the job!

Understanding the Word. Hebrews now makes the connection. Just as an earthly high priest could not just become a high priest, Jesus could not be a High Priest just because he wanted to be or because we wanted him to be. To be High Priest, Jesus would need to be called and appointed by God.

And so he was. Not only did God the Father call Jesus to be a priest from among humanity. Jesus was God himself come down to earth. As some later Christian thinkers would suggest, humanity was the one that had the problem that needed solving, but God was the only one who could solve it. How appropriate, then, that God would become human so that God could solve the problem that humanity needed solved.

In the Old Testament, Aaron was the first high priest. He did not become high priest because of an election or because he volunteered. Aaron did not run for the office. He became high priest by a divine appointment. God designated him as high priest. Then God designated his descendants as priests. So only Israelites who descended from Aaron and his ancestor Levi could serve as high priests.

Similarly, Jesus is not our High Priest just because he wanted to be. In fact, neither Aaron nor any of the high priests of the Old Testament could have been a priest like Jesus just because they wanted to be. God appointed Jesus as a unique kind of High Priest, a priest "after the order of Melchizedek." We will learn more about this kind of priest when we get to Hebrews 7. Suffice it to say, Jesus is the only High Priest of this sort to ever exist. Even Melchizedek himself, who was a model for such a priest, was not such a priest.

Hebrews quotes two key psalms in these verses in chapter 5. The first one is Psalm 2:7 (ESV) "You are my Son." This psalm tells us about Jesus' appointment as King. If you remember, the author already quoted Psalm 2 in Hebrews 1. Some would thus say that, up to this point in Hebrews, the author has been thinking primarily about Jesus as God's Son.

Now Hebrews goes on to quote another psalm. The second psalm quoted is Psalm 110:4 (ESV) "You are a priest forever." This is the verse that tells us about Jesus' appointment as priest. Jesus is the only person in all of history who has held these two appointments, and he holds them both forever. So now Hebrews moves from talking of Jesus as Son to Jesus as High Priest.

We, therefore, do not need to seek another king. We already have a ruler. God uses earthly kings and authorities, but they are far from perfect. In fact, more often than not they are perverse. They have often been evil. Even when our lives are comfortable and we are happy with those in authority over us, we must remember that our true "citizenship is in heaven" (Phil. 3:20).

We do not need to seek another priest either. We would be foolish even to think such a thing. Jesus is our King and Priest forever. He has done the deed. No other sacrifice is required.

1. Have you ever tried to take a role for yourself that really belonged to someone else, especially God?

2. In what ways might we subtly try to substitute some other king or priest for Jesus in our lives?

3. What would it mean if the world accepted Jesus as its true King and Priest?

FOUR

Source of Salvation

Hebrews 5:7–10 ESV *In the days of his flesh, Jesus offered up prayers and supplications, with loud cries and tears, to him who was able to save him from death, and he was heard because of his reverence. ⁸Although he was a son, he learned obedience through what he suffered. ⁹And being made perfect, he became the source of eternal salvation to all who obey him, ¹⁰being designated by God a high priest after the order of Melchizedek.*

Key Observation. If we think we should not have to endure suffering for God, we need only remember that Jesus was obedient and suffered too.

Understanding the Word. At first glance, you might be a little puzzled by these verses. Was Jesus not perfect at some point? Did Jesus need to learn obedience? What exactly is the author saying here?

The key to remember is that the author is sending a message to the congregation, a congregation facing difficult times. The point of these comments is not just to tell us interesting things about Jesus. This is not a theology lecture in a class. Hebrews is telling its audience these things because they are important for the nitty-gritty of their life at this moment. The imagery is deeply relevant to them.

Just because they are God's children does not mean that they will never suffer. You could argue that it is not good parenting to shield your children from all challenges. If a parent does everything for a child, how will the child survive when the parent is no longer around? Life is full of pain and injustice. We do not want to watch our children suffer, but at some point we need to let them grow up and mature.

Jesus was God's Son, just as those in the audience were God's children. Yet Jesus suffered and chose to obey and continued to follow God through hard times. So also they must choose to obey and follow God through hard times. In Hebrews 12, the author will remind them that discipline is not a bad thing. Without discipline, we would never be able to finish the race. We need the training.

We do not know for sure if the author of Hebrews had the garden of Gethsemane in mind when he wrote these verses, but many readers of Hebrews have certainly heard an echo of it. In Mark 14:36, Jesus asked God if it was possible for the cup of suffering to pass from him. Jesus clearly would rather not die on the cross.

Yet Jesus obediently followed through. He took the next step of faith, then the next step of faith. Sometimes being faithful only requires us not to run away, as Jesus might have easily run away at one point. But he stayed put. He stayed in the zone of persecution and suffering. His opponents and the Romans did the rest.

So also this congregation must decide whether to obediently move forward in faithfulness, regardless of the outcome, or to disobey and turn away. They must decide whether to take the next step in faith or not. They must decide whether to endure what is coming or to run away.

In the garden, Jesus struggled "with loud cries and tears" (v. 7), but he knew that God could save him out of death. His prayer for resurrection was answered because of his reverent obedience to God. So if this church will endure to the end, God will also grant them eternal life.

As in Hebrews 2, Jesus' perfection does not mean that he was imperfect before or that he had sinned before. "Perfect" in this context means "complete." In order to offer eternal atonement, it was fitting for Jesus to die for sins first. He was thus *ready* to atone, *ready* to serve as High Priest, after he had died and entered into the heavenly sanctuary.

1. Have you ever questioned why God was allowing you to endure some trial or suffering? Have you ever thought of what Jesus obediently endured in that moment?

2. If God ever tied the answers to our prayers to our reverent obedience, how many of our prayers would get answered? Thankfully, he is much more merciful than this!

3. Do we offer "loud cries and tears" for others? If God's action sometimes depends on our prayers, would we pray more often and more vigorously?

FIVE

Time to Grow Up

Hebrews 5:11–14 *We have much to say about this, but it is hard to make it clear to you because you no longer try to understand.* ¹²*In fact, though by this time you ought to be teachers, you need someone to teach you the elementary truths of God's word all over again. You need milk, not solid food!* ¹³*Anyone who lives on milk, being still an infant, is not acquainted with the teaching about righteousness.* ¹⁴*But solid food is for the mature, who by constant use have trained themselves to distinguish good from evil.*

Key Observation. We should not stand still in our faith after we believe in Christ. We should be more spiritually mature and able to withstand more temptation and opposition the longer we have been with Christ.

Understanding the Word. At this point, Hebrews interrupts its train of thought again to warn the church of its need to continue in faith. We have seen two of these interruptions so far. The first was at the beginning of chapter 2, after showing that Jesus was greater than the angels. The second was in Hebrews 3, after showing that Jesus was greater than Moses. Here, the author is in the middle of argument that Jesus is a greater priest than any earthly priest.

Hebrews 5:11–6:8 is the strongest of all the warnings in this sermon. It seems significant that it is the mention of Jesus as High Priest that sparks this warning. Given the chapters that follow, it is very likely that one of the biggest reasons for the church's doubt had to do with atonement. They just were not sure that Jesus had taken care of all their sins.

As we look back, it seems obvious that Jesus has taken care of our need for animal sacrifice. The Jewish temple has been gone for almost two thousand years. There has been no animal sacrifice among Jews for as many years. I have never seen an animal sacrifice and would have to travel to some obscure location in the world to find one. It is easy for me to believe that we need no temple or sacrifice any more.

But this was not the case at the time of the New Testament. The language in these verses is strong, even though the author will soften his tone in a moment. He was making a point in a strong, culturally appropriate way. It was appropriate rhetorically in the first century to overstate your case and move the audience in the right direction.

There is a little bit of shame in these words. The author told the audience that they should know better by then. They have been Christians for a long time. What was wrong with them? They should have been teaching such things by then. They should have known that they never needed to worry about atonement. Jesus had taken care of it. They did not need the temple in Jerusalem or the synagogue in town. Jesus paid it all.

Apart from these specifics, we learn from these verses that a Christian should grow spiritually over the years. Some Christians may struggle with certain temptations when they are young in faith. Some Christians may be troubled by lesser challenges when they first come to faith. But if we have been Christ-followers for a while, we should not still be struggling with the same temptations of our Christian infancy.

As we grow, we should be able to handle more significant challenges. And as we face them, we should find it easier and easier to overcome them. A pattern of complete surrender should become part of who we are. If twenty years later we are still where we were at first, then something is significantly wrong!

In particular, we should be able to tell the difference between good and evil. We should be able to tell the difference between what is of the Holy Spirit and what is of the devil. It is not always the case, unfortunately.

1. Have you grown since you first believed on Christ? Can you handle more opposition than at first? Is it easy to resist things that would have brought strong temptation before?

2. Can you see growth as a church over the years? Is there a core group of believers who have come for a long time and who collectively provide wisdom and strength for any challenge?

3. Does the world outside your church see something different about your church that they don't see in other places? Can they tell you are Christians by your love?

WEEK FOUR

GATHERING DISCUSSION OUTLINE

A. Open session in prayer.

B. View video for this week's readings.

C. What general impressions and thoughts do you have after considering the video and reading the daily writings on these Scriptures? How have you grown deeper in your faith and understanding of Scripture?

D. Discuss questions selected from the daily readings.

    1. **KEY OBSERVATION:** In Jesus we have a helper who both knows our needs and eagerly wants to come to our aid when we need it.

    DISCUSSION QUESTION: Sometimes we do not really want help. We may want to solve our problems on our own. Are you willing to rely on Christ rather than on yourself?

    2. **KEY OBSERVATION:** The purpose of a priest is to intercede for people to God. Jesus is the only priest we need.

    DISCUSSION QUESTION: Does your church offer gifts and sacrifices to God for your community and the world?

    3. **KEY OBSERVATION:** Jesus is the only King and priest we will ever need. He remains them forever, and he is perfect at the job!

    DISCUSSION QUESTION: Have you ever tried to take a role for yourself that really belonged to someone else, especially God?

4. **KEY OBSERVATION:** If we think we should not have to endure suffering for God, we need only remember that Jesus was obedient and suffered too.

   DISCUSSION QUESTION: Have you ever questioned why God was allowing you to endure some trial or suffering? Have you ever thought of what Jesus obediently endured in that moment?

5. **KEY OBSERVATION:** We should not stand still in our faith after we believe in Christ. We should be more spiritually mature and able to withstand more temptation and opposition the longer we have been with Christ.

   DISCUSSION QUESTION: Can you see growth as a church over the years? Is there a core group of believers who have come for a long time and who collectively provide wisdom and strength for any challenge?

E. Close session with prayer.

WEEK FIVE

Hebrews 6:1–20; 7:1–19

Don't Fall Away

INTRODUCTION

Hebrews 6 finishes up the author's warning that this church cannot turn its back on Christ now. In some of the strongest language in the sermon, the author warned that there would be no coming back if they were to leave Christ at this late stage of their spiritual walk. At the same time, he expressed his faith that they would not turn away. God keeps his promises, and they just needed to trust his word.

In Hebrews 7, the author returned to his argument that Christ is a priest from a different line than the priests who descended from Aaron and his ancestor Levi. He explained what a priest after the order of Melchizedek is and why they are superior to any priest from the line of Levi. Jesus turned out to be superior to yet another group from the old covenant. He is superior to the angels who delivered the Law to Moses, and he is superior to Moses. Now we learn that he is superior to all the priests of the old covenant.

ONE

Point of No Return

Hebrews 6:4–6 NRSV *For it is impossible to restore again to repentance those who have once been enlightened, and have tasted the heavenly gift, and have shared in the Holy Spirit, ⁵and have tasted the goodness of the word of God and the powers of the age to come, ⁶and then have fallen away, since on their own they are crucifying again the Son of God and are holding him up to contempt.*

Key Observation. Our hearts can become so hard that we reach a point of no return, from which we cannot get back.

Understanding the Word. These verses are some of the most controversial ones in the Bible. They are difficult for one group of Christians because they seem to say that you can stop being a Christian. To another group they are difficult because they seem to say that once you stop, you cannot come back.

On the one hand, Hebrews is almost certainly warning people who are truly Christians. Even though the author used words like "tasting" and "sharing," he used these words elsewhere of Jesus tasting death (2:9) and sharing flesh and blood (2:14). They are not words he used for someone who did not fully embrace something.

We should assume that those he had in mind were fully Christian. These were not people who had just gone to church once or twice and not returned. These were not half-hearted church attenders. Perhaps some would argue that those who did not persist only appeared to be believers. In this way of thinking, they were never truly believers in the first place. If this is the case, Hebrews certainly does not say so.

Nor does this warning seem to be an idle threat. It is true that the author did not think that the audience would fall away in the end (6:9). Nevertheless, we have every reason to think that falling away is a real possibility. What is the point of making such a warning if it can never actually happen? To do so seems deceptive—misleading, at the very best.

On the other side, some have argued that the use of the present tense ("it *is* impossible," "to be renewing") means that, in the moment of falling away, they are truly separated from God in that moment. This interpretation is attractive because it would say nothing about coming back to God at a future point in time. Unfortunately, this line of thinking seems to stretch the grammar beyond what it will bear.

Other scholars suggest that this is a sin that none of us today could commit. The line of thinking here is that this congregation was so close to Jesus in time and space, they had so much knowledge. How could someone come back after turning away from such knowledge?

These verses do give us one picture of what it means to become a Christian. A Christian is someone who has received the Holy Spirit, as we learn also in both Acts (e.g., 2:28) and Romans (e.g., 8:9). To receive the Holy Spirit is to get a sense of what the powers of the coming age will be like (cf. 2 Cor. 1:22).

However, this atonement does not give us unlimited license to do whatever we want. We can, in effect, crucify Jesus again by abandoning him. Repentance is not so easy to find if we go so far. We will see the frightening image of Esau later in Hebrews, who could not find a place of repentance, even though he sought it diligently (12:17).

We know from elsewhere in the Bible that God will take us back no matter how far we stray. The parable of the prodigal son (Luke 15:11–32) presents this truth clearly. The problem is that if our heart gets hard enough, we may not be able to repent, even though we realize we need to. When you have as much knowledge as the church of Hebrews and are so close to Christ himself, falling away seems a point of no return.

1. Some people need peace and assurance about the security of their salvation. Others take their salvation for granted when they are not really committed to Christ. Do you fall into either of these categories?

2. How can the church speak assurance to those who need to be reassured and yet strongly encourage those who are not fully committed to Christ?

3. How horrible it is to think that someone might re-crucify Jesus by treating his atoning death as a trivial thing! How can we make sure that our lives never do such a thing?

TWO

I Believe in You

Hebrews 6:9–12 *Even though we speak like this, dear friends, we are convinced of better things in your case—the things that have to do with salvation.* [10] *God is not unjust; he will not forget your work and the love you have shown him as you have helped his people and continue to help them.* [11] *We want each of you to show this same diligence to the very end, so that what you hope for may be fully realized.* [12] *We do not want you to become lazy, but to imitate those who through faith and patience inherit what has been promised.*

Key Observation. Our past victories are milestones of faith that remind us that we can make it going forward because God is with us today just like he was with us in the past.

Understanding the Word. The stern warning of yesterday's verses continues in Hebrews 6:7–8. The author warned about how a field that only yields thorns and thistles after God has repeatedly provided rain is a field that is destined for burning. His point is clear enough. If God gives and gives to a person—or in this case a community—but the land refuses to yield fruit, God will eventually abandon that land.

And since it is the Holy Spirit that empowers us to come to God in the first place, we simply will not come to God if he has left us. This is an important point. As long as we feel the longing to be reconciled to God, then God's Holy Spirit has not abandoned us. This fact means that anyone who truly wants to return to God can. If it is possible to apostatize after being a true believer, then you will never truly long to return.

But the author did not think that that church faced this fate. He saw where the trajectory of doubt and apostasy could lead. It was a road that the audience was flirting with in their sluggish faith. But he did not believe they would continue on the path that far. They had shown their faith in the past (cf. 10:32–35), and the author was convinced that they would show their faith again.

When the moment of decision truly came, the author was convinced they would step forward in faith. If they were arrested, they would remain faithful. If believers were imprisoned, they would bring them food and other things prisoners might need. Sometimes we are not sure of ourselves. We see a choice of obedience approaching and perhaps we are not entirely sure what we will do. This is a point where others can come alongside us and give us the strength to do the right thing. Accountability, while not always pleasant in the moment, is a gift to those of us who are earnestly following Christ.

Meanwhile, God had not forgotten them. God remembered their faithfulness before. God was not going to abandon them now in this time of crisis. As Hebrews says later, God would never leave them nor forsake them (13:5). When we face these moments, we know that the Holy Spirit is with us to strengthen us and pull us through.

But at that moment, they had become lazy in their faith. They had grown tired of the struggle. They needed to regain their focus and get reenergized.

They needed to be like those who inherit God's promises. They needed to be like the heroes of faith that the author will remind them about in Hebrews 11.

God still believed in them. The author of Hebrews still believed in them. A cloud of witnesses from the Old Testament stood as a testimony to God's faithfulness. The fact that the book of Hebrews is in the New Testament suggests that they did continue in faith through whatever trial they were facing.

1. Are there victorious milestones in your personal faith that you can look back on to become inspired to keep moving forward in faith?

2. Are there milestones in the life of your community of faith that inspire your church to move forward into the future?

3. Are there points in the story of your church where you have been a powerful witness to the community outside the church? They could be moments of suffering or evangelism or service.

THREE

God Doesn't Lie

Hebrews 6:17–20 ESV *So when God desired to show more convincingly to the heirs of the promise the unchangeable character of his purpose, he guaranteed it with an oath, [18]so that by two unchangeable things, in which it is impossible for God to lie, we who have fled for refuge might have strong encouragement to hold fast to the hope set before us. [19]We have this as a sure and steadfast anchor of the soul, a hope that enters into the inner place behind the curtain, [20]where Jesus has gone as a forerunner on our behalf . . .*

Key Observation. God's promise to bring salvation stands secure because God has sworn it and cannot lie.

Understanding the Word. After his strong warning about falling away and after expressing his confidence that the audience would not fall away, the last part of Hebrews 6 reassured this church that God is dependable. They should not doubt God's promises, because God has done more than promise. God has sworn with an oath that he will do as he promised.

We do not take oaths very seriously today, but oaths were very significant in the times of the Bible. In fact, the command not to take God's name in vain was originally about taking oaths in God's name. If you made such an oath, it was very serious indeed, and you would have to answer to God if you invoked his name and did not follow through!

You might remember the story of Jephthah from Judges 11. He made a vow in the name of the Lord that he would sacrifice the first living thing that came out of his house if God would grant him victory in battle. That first living thing turned out to be his daughter, and Jephthah went on to sacrifice her. This story is just a small indication of how seriously the taking of oaths was in the biblical world.

The fact that God has sworn that Jesus is a priest in Psalm 110:4 is thus a point of incredible assurance. You did not swear about something that is not true or you would face certain judgment and catastrophe. The fact that God has taken an oath is a sure indicator that his promise will come true.

A second point of assurance is the fact that God does not lie. God is a God of the truth, and everything that is true coheres with God. As the saying goes, "All truth is God's truth."

We can thus be sure that God is going to fix what is wrong in the world, because he has told us so. He does not lie. We can be sure that our sins are taken care of. We can be sure that Jesus is coming again to set up his kingdom.

Hebrews paints several pictures to reinforce this great security. One is that of an Old Testament city of refuge. These were cities designated for those who had accidentally caused someone's death. As long as you stayed in this city, you were safe. So also we who believe have refuge in God, no matter what is happening around us. We are safe. We do not need to keep an eye out for some other outcome. The outcome is certain. God will give us eternal protection.

The second image is that of an anchor. Despite the waves of their world, the audience has an anchor that will keep them steadfast. Storms may come, but our ship will stay intact and our ship will stay in place.

Finally, Jesus has gone as High Priest into the highest heaven itself, guaranteeing our reconciliation with God. After these warnings and assurances, the author skillfully returned to the topic that launched this warning in 5:11. He returned to the high priesthood of Jesus.

1. How easily do you trust in God's promises in Scripture? How well do you trust that God is one day going to set the world straight?

2. Is your church a place of refuge for those who are being beaten by the waves of the world and its struggles?

3. Would not the world around us love to have an anchor to help weather the storms of life? Do those within your church's reach see you and it as potential anchors for their souls?

FOUR
A Priest like Melchizedek

Hebrews 7:1–3 NRSV *This "King Melchizedek of Salem, priest of the Most High God, met Abraham as he was returning from defeating the kings and blessed him"; ²and to him Abraham apportioned "one-tenth of everything." His name, in the first place, means "king of righteousness"; next he is also king of Salem, that is, "king of peace." ³Without father, without mother, without genealogy, having neither beginning of days nor end of life, but resembling the Son of God, he remains a priest forever.*

Key Observation. Jesus did not come from a priestly line. He has existed from eternity past and will continue as priest forever.

Understanding the Word. Hebrews 7 picks up right where the author left off his argument in 5:10. In chapter 5, the author reminded this church what a priest was and how a person came to be one. He told them that Jesus became a priest after the order of Melchizedek. Jesus was obedient to death and then saved out of death because he was faithful to God. In chapter 7 he explained what a priest after the order of Melchizedek actually is.

Where did the author's interest in Melchizedek come from? It no doubt started in Psalm 110. In the Gospels, Jesus himself connected the first verse of this psalm to himself, the Messiah. The Lord—God the Father—said to our Lord Jesus Christ, "Sit at my right hand." The earliest Christians referred to this verse often. They understood Psalm 110:1 to predict that God would install Jesus as King after his resurrection.

It was only natural to connect the fourth verse of Psalm 110 to Jesus as well. It says that the Messiah is a priest after the order of Melchizedek. This fact raised the question for the author, "What exactly is a priest after the order of Melchizedek?"

To answer this question, the author turned to the only other place in the Old Testament where Melchizedek is mentioned—Genesis 14. In this chapter, Abraham had gone to war to rescue his nephew Lot and was returning from battle with the spoils of victory. As he returned he met a priest of the "most high God" (v. 18 KJV) (*El Elyon* in Hebrew). In the days of Abraham, since God was not yet known by the name Yahweh, "Most High God" was one of the best ways they knew to refer to him—he is the highest God.

So Abraham met this priest of the Most High God when returning from battle. Abraham gave Melchizedek a tenth (or tithe) of all the spoils of war (see Genesis 14:20). In return, Melchizedek blessed Abraham.

Some have wondered if Melchizedek might have been Christ himself. In fact, this was a very popular thought throughout the centuries. But it may simply be that Hebrews saw a picture of Christ in the way Genesis described this ancient priest. Hebrews gave a spiritual interpretation of the story of Melchizedek.

For example, take the name Melchizedek. In the Hebrew language, it has two parts that mean "king" and "righteousness." The author of Hebrews concluded that a priest after the order of Melchizedek would be a righteous king. He is the king of Salem, which is the word for *shalom*, or peace. A priest after the order of Melchizedek would be a king of peace.

The author also noted that Genesis never said anything about when Melchizedek became priest or stopped being priest. The story never mentioned Melchizedek coming from a family of priests. A priest in the order of Melchizedek would not come from a priestly genealogy and will remain a priest forever. Jesus did not come from a priestly line. He has existed from eternity past and will continue as priest forever.

1. Have you ever sensed the Lord speaking to you through Scripture in a way that seemed to go beyond what the text was originally saying? What are the benefits and dangers of reading the Bible this way?

2. How are pastors different today than they were in the time of Jesus and Melchizedek? What has changed?

3. Have you ever contemplated how much more we know about God, because we have the Bible, than someone like Abraham did three thousand years ago? Give thanks to God for this great privilege!

FIVE

A Priest Forever

Hebrews 7:15–19 *And what we have said is even more clear if another priest like Melchizedek appears, ¹⁶one who has become a priest not on the basis of a regulation as to his ancestry but on the basis of the power of an indestructible life. ¹⁷For it is declared: "You are a priest forever, in the order of Melchizedek."*

¹⁸The former regulation is set aside because it was weak and useless ¹⁹(for the law made nothing perfect), and a better hope is introduced, by which we draw near to God.

Key Observation. We can rely on Jesus entirely to take care of our sins, and through him we can truly come into God's presence.

Understanding the Word. In the verses between yesterday's scripture and today, the author of Hebrews established that a priest after the order of Melchizedek was superior to a Levitical priest who might serve in the earthly sanctuary. First, Melchizedek blessed Abraham, and Abraham gave tithes to Melchizedek. These events clearly show who was superior to whom. The superior blessed the inferior, and the inferior gave a portion to the superior.

Melchizedek was thus superior to Abraham. When we realize that Levi was the grandson of Abraham, we see that Levi was also inferior to Melchizedek, because he was, in a sense, "in the loins" of Abraham when Melchizedek blessed Abraham. The author thus concluded that a priest after the order of Melchizedek was superior to one who was in the order of Levi.

Hebrews then asks, if the Levitical priesthood were sufficient, why does Psalm 110 speak of a king-priest like Melchizedek who was yet to come? Why is the Messiah a priest if the Levitical priests who served in the temple in Jerusalem were adequate? Hebrews concludes that the system of earthly priests and earthly sacrifices simply was not able to make an Israelite whole.

"Perfection"—cleansing from sin and a restoration to wholeness—simply did not come through the priests who descended from Levi.

The author then went one step further. If there is a change of priesthood because Christ has come as a king-priest of a superior order, then there will also be a change of law. The sacrificial law of the Old Testament, he said, was no longer necessary. He will develop this idea further in the next few chapters. The sacrifices of the old covenant were something like place holders. They did not actually work to take away sins. Now that Christ has died for sins, they are no longer needed.

Now we get to the verses for today. The reason why Christ's priesthood is the final priesthood is because he has an indestructible life. He never will stop being a priest, unlike the earthly priests from the tribe of Levi. Their priestly rules were weak and ineffective. The priesthood of Christ actually makes it possible to draw near to God. As it says later in the chapter, Jesus "is able to save completely those who come to God through him, because he always lives to intercede for them" (7:25).

The chapter ends with a celebration of Jesus as priest, who is "holy, blameless, pure, set apart from sinners, exalted above the heavens" (7:26). Why would we worry a moment about needing another priest when we have this One who made a once-and-for-all sacrifice? He has been made perfect as a priest forever.

Hebrews 7 is a somewhat complicated argument, but the basic point is clear. We can rely on Jesus as our priest. We do not have to worry about the atonement that the temple seemed to provide, because it did not really provide that atonement. We can rely on Jesus entirely to take care of our sins, and through him we can truly come into God's presence.

1. Since Hebrews was written to people in a different time and place, we should not be surprised if its argument may sound a little strange to us. How would you express the argument of Hebrews 7 to someone today?

2. Do you ever try to rely on solutions that are only passing, rather than counting on the more permanent solutions that may be harder than the quick fix?

3. Are there priests that non-believers sometimes count on when they could count on the priest to end all priests? How can you show them a more perfect way?

WEEK FIVE

GATHERING DISCUSSION OUTLINE

A. Open session in prayer.

B. View video for this week's readings.

C. What general impressions and thoughts do you have after considering the video and reading the daily writings on these Scriptures? How have you grown deeper in your faith and understanding of Scripture?

D. Discuss questions selected from the daily readings.

    1. **KEY OBSERVATION:** Our hearts can become so hard that we reach a point of no return, from which we cannot get back.

    DISCUSSION QUESTION: How can the church speak assurance to those who need to be reassured and yet strongly encourage those who are not fully committed to Christ?

    2. **KEY OBSERVATION:** Our past victories are milestones of faith that remind us that we can make it going forward because God is with us today just like he was with us in the past.

    DISCUSSION QUESTION: Are there victorious milestones in your personal faith that you can look back on to become inspired to keep moving forward in faith?

    3. **KEY OBSERVATION:** God's promise to bring salvation stands secure because God has sworn it and cannot lie.

DISCUSSION QUESTION: Would not the world around us love to have an anchor to help weather the storms of life? Do those within your church's reach see you and it as potential anchors for their souls?

4. **KEY OBSERVATION:** Jesus did not come from a priestly line. He has existed from eternity past and will continue as priest forever.

   DISCUSSION QUESTION: Have you ever sensed the Lord speaking to you through Scripture in a way that seemed to go beyond what the text was originally saying? What are the benefits and dangers of reading the Bible this way?

5. **KEY OBSERVATION:** We can rely on Jesus entirely to take care of our sins, and through him we can truly come into God's presence.

   DISCUSSION QUESTION: Do you ever try to rely on solutions that are only passing, rather than counting on the more permanent solutions that may be harder than the quick fix?

E. Close session with prayer.

Hebrews 8:5–10; 9:7–28

The Perfect Sanctuary and Sacrifice

INTRODUCTION

In Hebrews 5, the author told us the basic purpose of a high priest. In Hebrews 7, the author explained what a priest after the order of Melchizedek is and why such a priest is superior to any Old Testament priest. Now that such a priest has arrived—Jesus—there is no need for the Old Testament sacrificial system at all.

The next few chapters (8:1–10:18) get down to the nitty-gritty. The old covenant is now obsolete. The old animal sacrifices are no longer necessary. This fact implies that the sacrificial system of Jerusalem is now unnecessary. In Hebrews 8, the author focuses on the change of covenant that is now taking place. The old covenant is now obsolete. A new covenant is arriving. Then, Hebrews 9 shows how both the sacrifice of Jesus and the heavenly sanctuary are superior to earthly sacrifices and the earthly sanctuary.

ONE

The Heavenly Tent

Hebrews 8:5–6 NRSV *They offer worship in a sanctuary that is a sketch and shadow of the heavenly one; for Moses, when he was about to erect the tent, was warned, "See that you make everything according to the pattern that was shown you on the mountain." ⁶But Jesus has now obtained a more excellent ministry, and to that degree he is the mediator of a better covenant, which has been enacted through better promises.*

Key Observation. The only thing we need in order to be reconciled with God is the death and life of Jesus Christ.

Understanding the Word. In Hebrews 7, the author showed that Jesus is a superior priest to any earthly priest of the Old Testament. In Hebrews 8–9, we will see that Jesus is a superior sacrifice offered in a superior sanctuary. Hebrews 8 actually begins with a summary of the author's main teaching point: "we have such a high priest, one who is seated at the right hand of the throne of the Majesty in the heavens, a minister in the sanctuary and the true tent that the Lord, and not any mortal, has set up" (8:1–2 NRSV).

The point the author was making is that no earthly sanctuary could ever do anything but foreshadow or illustrate the true sanctuary, which is the heavenly place where God's throne is. Experts on Hebrews debate the exact nature of this heavenly sanctuary. Many translations of Hebrews 8:5 make this heavenly temple sound like something from a philosophy class. The Greek philosopher Plato suggested that everything on earth was a copy and a shadow of the real version in heaven.

It is not a bad way to think of what Hebrews is saying. The early sanctuary was never meant to be the real deal. It was always patterned after a much greater reality in heaven where God's presence exists in its fullness.

Others suggest that the author of Hebrews was really referring to a building in heaven. My own preference is that the author is referring to heaven itself (9:24) as the heavenly sanctuary. Many Jews at the time of Christ thought that, as you ascended upward, you went through layers of sky until you reached the highest heaven where God's throne was. I like to think that the author of Hebrews was talking of this highest heaven as the true Most Holy Place in the sanctuary to end all sanctuaries.

Whichever option the author had in mind, the earthly sanctuary was constructed in such a way as to make us think of the true, heavenly one. After leaving Egypt, Moses constructed the first sanctuary in the desert according to a pattern that God showed him, and that pattern was meant to cause Israel to reflect on the true one where God was.

Now that Jesus was serving in that true sanctuary, it was clear that the need for the first covenant had now ended. The promise of the first covenant was that Christ would soon come and offer definitive atonement for sins. The better promise of the new covenant was to have actual cleansing and forgiveness for them.

We do not know for sure what was troubling the church to which Hebrews was written. Were they feeling excluded in some way from the Jerusalem temple? Had the temple recently been destroyed, leaving them wondering how they would find atonement for their sins? Were they being excluded from the local synagogue in some way?

Different experts have different ideas. But what we do know is that Christ's death and life was the answer. They had no need for any of these things because Christ himself had settled our bill with God. Nothing on earth can substitute for God, who is what is most real of everything that exists.

1. Do you have a sense of your need for atonement, your need for some peace offering between yourself and God? If the audience of Hebrews was uncertain how to find atonement, we today may not fully realize our need for it in the first place.

2. What are the better promises that Christ brings to the church?

3. What are the better promises that Christ brings to the world?

TWO

A New Covenant

Hebrews 8:7–8, 10b *For if there had been nothing wrong with that first covenant, no place would have been sought for another. ⁸But God found fault with the people and said: "The days are coming, declares the Lord, when I will make a new covenant with the people of Israel and with the people of Judah. . . . ¹⁰I will put my laws in their minds and write them on their hearts. I will be their God, and they will be my people."*

Key Observation. Because of the blood of Jesus Christ, God now writes his law on our hearts through the Holy Spirit, empowering us to love one another.

Understanding the Word. At first glance, it may sound like Hebrews is saying that the only reason for a new covenant is because the first covenant failed. It is true that Israel failed God repeatedly in the Old Testament, just as so many of God's people have failed him throughout history. The book of Judges is one story of failure after failure, followed by repentance and restoration.

But it is clear from the rest of this section of the sermon that the author was not saying such a thing. God had planned for Jesus to come since the creation of the world (e.g., 9:26). The sacrifices of the Old Testament were never expected to take away sins for real (e.g., 10:1–2). They always pointed forward to Christ's one-time death and new life. Although Israel did fail God on numerous occasions, their failure alone was not the reason for Christ's coming.

In this passage, the author turned to Jeremiah 31 for a word from God in an earlier era. At that time, the northern kingdom had already been destroyed for almost 150 years. We call the tribes from the north the "lost tribes of Israel," because the Assyrians so scattered them to the winds. When Jeremiah was prophesying, the southern kingdom had just been defeated and Jerusalem destroyed.

It is against this backdrop that God gave these words to Jeremiah, which Hebrews repeats in what is the longest quotation from the Old Testament recorded in the New Testament. Israel was no doubt disheartened and discouraged. Who would not be? It might look like this was the end. They had failed God and they might have thought he had destroyed them forever.

But in Jeremiah 31, God gave hope to the Jews for the future. He did not plan to leave them captive in Babylon forever (Jer. 29:11). At some future point, God would make a new covenant with them. In this new covenant, God would write his laws on their hearts. They would not need to follow a path that they read about or heard about. God's will was going to be inside them. God would write his commandments on their hearts, and his commandment is for us to love our neighbor.

Jesus inaugurated that new covenant. Jesus took away the sins that the Law could not. Jesus made it possible for God's law to be written on our hearts.

As Christians, we believe that God writes his law on our hearts through the Holy Spirit. The Spirit of Christ within us is not only a Spirit that adopts us into God's family, whether we are Jews or non-Jews. The Spirit also empowers us to have love for one another, which fulfills the Old Testament Law. The Spirit produces the fruit in our lives of "love, joy, peace, patience, kindness, goodness, faithfulness, gentleness, and self-control" (Gal. 5:22–23 ESV).

Although the old covenant was good and pointed Israel to Christ, the new covenant far surpasses it. The old covenant was particular to one people; the new covenant is available to all people. The old covenant told God's people how they should live; the new covenant empowers us to keep God's commandment, which is to love one another.

1. Do you sense that God's law is written on your heart? If not, ask the Holy Spirit to come on you in a way that he has never come before!

2. Does your community of faith manifest the fruits of the Spirit—love, joy, peace, patience, kindness, goodness, faithfulness, gentleness, and self-control? If not, why not start a small group to pray for God to bring revival in your community?

3. What would happen if the communities outside of our churches saw us living with God's law written on our hearts? What would happen in the world?

THREE

The Most Holy Place

Hebrews 9:7–9a ESV *but into the second [room] only the high priest goes, and he but once a year, and not without taking blood, which he offers for himself and for the unintentional sins of the people. [8]By this the Holy Spirit indicates that the way into the holy places is not yet opened as long as the first section is still standing[9](which is symbolic for the present age).*

Key Observation. The two rooms of the sanctuary of Israel can be taken to symbolize two ages of history. In the age of Christ, there is no need for continual animal sacrifice because God has removed the outer room.

Understanding the Word. Hebrews 8 ends with the claim that the old covenant was now almost gone. Experts disagree whether this comment means that the temple had already been destroyed. Some think everyone would have known the old covenant was over if the temple was already destroyed when the author of Hebrews wrote these words. There are a number of places in these middle chapters where the author referred to the sacrificial system in the present tense.

But that is probably only our hindsight. At the time, they did not know how long the temple would lie in ruins. A number of authors from the decades after the destruction of the Jerusalem temple continued to refer to its operations in the present tense. My own sense is that the destruction of the temple itself was actually what made it possible to see that the old covenant was obsolete and passing away.

Hebrews 9 then begins an allegory based on the two parts of the Old Testament sanctuary. First, the author described the two rooms of that earthly tent that Israel carried around with them during their wanderings in the desert for forty years (9:1–5). There was a first room, called the "Holy Place," and there was a second room called the "Most Holy Place."

It is interesting that Hebrews does not actually call them rooms, but two "tents." The author probably talked about the rooms this way to get us ready for the point he was moving toward—God has removed the first tent, the first age, the first covenant. By treating the two parts of the earthly sanctuary as distinct structures, he highlighted their differences and separation.

He tells us what items were in the first room; namely, the lampstand and the table with consecrated bread. Some Jews interpreted these items symbolically, although the author of Hebrews does not do so here. Then he tells us that the second room had a golden altar of incense and the ark of the covenant. Here he differs a little from Exodus 30, which places the altar of incense in the first room. However, the altar of incense only received blood once a year (Exod. 30:10), which may be why Hebrews associates it with the Most Holy Place. It is also possible that the incense represents the prayers of God's people. In that case, the altar of incense is something we symbolically use even in the new covenant.

The verse for today takes the structure of the earthly sanctuary symbolically and spiritually. Yes, there was a literal structure, but the most important takeaway from it for us is not literal. It is the fact that God is removing the first room, which represents the old covenant with its never-ending sacrifices. Instead, God is symbolically establishing the second room, the once-and-for-all room.

Priests went into the first room over and over again, continually. Only the high priest went into the second room once a year. Jesus' sacrifice is a once-and-for-all sacrifice, so there is no need for an earthly sanctuary any more. A new age has come. The age of the Most Holy Place.

1. You might get a sense that the removal of the outer room suggests that the way for us to holiness has now become open in Jesus. Do you see in Jesus a path to become more like God?

2. While we are often tempted to think of our relationship with God as an individual thing, the High Priest entered the sanctuary for all the people. In what ways can we become a holy people for God together?

3. First Peter 2:5 calls the church "a holy priesthood." How can we be priests who intercede to God for the world?

FOUR

The Effective Sacrifice

Hebrews 9:11–14 NRSV *But when Christ came as a high priest of the good things that have come, . . . ¹²he entered once for all into the Holy Place, not with the blood of goats and calves, but with his own blood, thus obtaining eternal redemption. ¹³For if the blood of goats and bulls, with the sprinkling of the ashes of a heifer, sanctifies those who have been defiled so that their flesh is purified, ¹⁴how much more will the blood of Christ, who through the eternal Spirit offered himself without blemish to God, purify our conscience from dead works to worship the living God!*

Key Observation. God still wants to cleanse us today from the things we have done that would otherwise lead to eternal death.

Understanding the Word. These verses continue the same point that we looked at in the previous devotional. Christ entered into the Most Holy Place once, and that was enough. The blood of animals was not sufficient. Goats, calves, and bulls could not take away our sins, as we will see when we get to Hebrews 10. It took Christ's blood to do the job. And once Christ's blood had done the job, there was no need for anyone to ever sacrifice blood again.

We see several types of Old Testament sacrifice in these verses. You may never have noticed the ceremony in Numbers 19 where the ashes of a red heifer were put in water and used to cleanse individuals of uncleanness. Hebrews alludes to that ceremony here. What the author of Hebrews was doing was showing that there is no sacrifice in the Old Testament that Jesus' blood does not replace. His blood is so effective that none of these earlier ceremonies need ever be done again. He has taken care of them with his own blood.

In Hebrews, to sanctify a person especially means to cleanse someone of sin. When we are sanctified, we are washed clean. To sanctify also had the more basic sense of setting someone apart as holy, as belonging to God. We are no longer common. We are no longer outside of God. The blood of Jesus could do this task, while Hebrews claims that the blood of no animal from the old covenant could.

Christ was a high priest "of the good things that have come" (9:11 NRSV). There is a verse in the next chapter that talks about how the Jewish Law had a shadow of good things to come. The good thing to come was the atonement provided by Christ, of which the Law only gave a foreshadowing by way of its animal sacrifices. Hebrews 10 will tell us that our consciences could not really become clear under the old covenant. But they can by way of Christ!

Some scholars of the Old Testament would say that the real power for cleansing in sacrifice was not so much in the death of the victim, but in the powerful life of the blood. As Leviticus 17:11 says, the life is in the blood. Imagine the power that Jesus' eternal Spirit brings for our forgiveness and cleansing. The blood of animals might cleanse our skin, but Jesus' Spirit has the power to cleanse our spirits.

Jesus is cleansing us from dead works so that we can truly worship the living God. What are these "dead works" (Heb. 9:14 NRSV)? It would be reading Hebrews out of context to think of these as "good works" instead of faith. The NIV probably catches the sense well when it translates the phrase, "acts that lead to death." Mention of the living God may remind this congregation that there were many in that world who worshipped idols, which were not alive like the God of Israel.

God can still cleanse us from the things we do today that lead to eternal death. Jesus' Spirit is a spirit of life from the dead. The power of his life can still give life to us, not only for eternity, but in our living from day to day now!

1. There is a reminder in these verses that we cannot cleanse ourselves. Indeed, religion cannot cleanse us. Have you relied on Christ for your cleansing?

2. Worship is fittingly done in community. What would it look like if we worshipped God not only as purified individuals but as a spotless and blameless church?

3. The blood of Christ gives life to all who experience his Spirit. How can we as a church bring life to our world because we touch it in Jesus' name?

FIVE

The Second Coming

Hebrews 9:26b–28 *But he has appeared once for all at the culmination of the ages to do away with sin by the sacrifice of himself.* [27]*Just as people are destined to die once, and after that to face judgment,* [28]*so Christ was sacrificed once to take away the sins of many; and he will appear a second time, not to bear sin, but to bring salvation to those who are waiting for him.*

Key Observation. The key takeaway for believers from these verses is not fear of judgment, but hope and joy at the prospect of salvation.

Understanding the Word. You may at some point have heard someone refer to the idea of Jesus' second coming. That phrase comes from these verses. Those of us here on earth will see Jesus appear "a second time." The first time he came was, of course, when he came to earth as a human in Galilee. He walked the earth for a little more than thirty years and showed us what it was like to be a complete and ideal human being. He showed us what it was like to live under the full power of the Holy Spirit and be victorious over temptation. Then he died for our sins and was raised to resurrection life just as we will live one day forever.

Christians believe that Jesus will come again. Some have reduced this idea to the notion that you die and then immediately either go to heaven or hell. It is understandable, given that God has allowed such a long period of time to pass between Jesus' first and second comings. Indeed, we believe that we do go to a place of reward or separation from God immediately when we die.

But Christians have historically believed that a day will come when Jesus will return and set up an eternal kingdom here on a new earth. The days of Christ's return are days of both salvation and judgment. For those who are not serving God, these will be unpleasant days, to say the least. The book of Revelation is largely symbolic in its images, but we get the picture clearly enough. Those who have rejected God do not face a happy future in the time of Christ's return.

By contrast, Christ will return for salvation to those who are following God and who have believed in Jesus as King. Salvation means rescue or escape from harm. Those who wait for Christ will not have to endure the judgment that is coming. First Thessalonians 4:16–17 speaks of how the dead in Christ will rise and come back with Christ. Then we who are alive at the time will join them in the air. Paul did not seem to think that we then go off to heaven but that we all then come down together for the judgment (cf. 1 Cor. 6:2–3).

It is clear that the author of Hebrews believed that we were living in the final days of history, the "culmination of the ages" (9:26). Jesus has ushered in the final act of the drama. The problem of history is solved. We are simply waiting for the solution to play itself out fully and finally.

Sin has been defeated and abolished. One of the reasons that the author of Hebrews was so hard on sin after coming to Christ is that Christ has taken care of sin. It did not make sense at all that those who trusted in Christ's death and resurrection would nail Jesus to the cross again.

These verses also give us a glimpse of what happens between death and the final judgment. There seems to be a temporary judgment immediately when we die. Most of the New Testament would not consider this judgment at death as the end. Revelation 20, in particular, suggests that there will be a definitive judgment for all the dead.

1. As an individual, do these verses not make us want to be certain that we are in that group of people who will rejoice to see Jesus return?

2. As a church, will we be delighted at Christ's return? Have we been operating in one spirit and as one, just as Jesus prayed in John 17:11 or as Paul urged the Philippians in Philippians 2:2?

3. If the world is facing the prospect of judgment, how much more urgently should we want as many people as possible to be ready?

WEEK SIX

GATHERING DISCUSSION OUTLINE

A. Open session in prayer.

B. View video for this week's readings.

C. What general impressions and thoughts do you have after considering the video and reading the daily writings on these Scriptures? How have you grown deeper in your faith and understanding of Scripture?

D. Discuss questions selected from the daily readings.

    1. **KEY OBSERVATION:** The only thing we need in order to be reconciled with God is the death and life of Jesus Christ.

    DISCUSSION QUESTION: Do you have a sense of your need for atonement, your need for some peace offering between yourself and God? If the audience of Hebrews was uncertain how to find atonement, we today may not fully realize our need for it in the first place.

    2. **KEY OBSERVATION:** Because of the blood of Jesus Christ, God now writes his law on our hearts through the Holy Spirit, empowering us to love one another.

    DISCUSSION QUESTION: Does your community of faith manifest the fruits of the Spirit—love, joy, peace, patience, kindness, goodness, faithfulness, gentleness, and self-control? If not, why not start a small group to pray for God to bring revival in your community?

3. **KEY OBSERVATION:** The two rooms of the sanctuary of Israel can be taken to symbolize two ages of history. In the age of Christ, there is no need for continual animal sacrifice because God has removed the outer room.

   DISCUSSION QUESTION: You might get a sense that the removal of the outer room suggests that the way for us to holiness has now become open in Jesus. Do you see in Jesus a path to become more like God?

4. **KEY OBSERVATION:** God still wants to cleanse us today from the things we have done that would otherwise lead to eternal death.

   DISCUSSION QUESTION: The blood of Christ gives life to all who experience his Spirit. How can we as a church bring life to our world because we touch it in Jesus' name?

5. **KEY OBSERVATION:** The key takeaway for believers from these verses is not fear of judgment, but hope and joy at the prospect of salvation.

   DISCUSSION QUESTION: As a church, will we be delighted at Christ's return? Have we been operating in one spirit and as one, just as Jesus prayed in John 17:11 or as Paul urged the Philippians in Philippians 2:2?

E. Close session with prayer.

WEEK SEVEN

Hebrews 10:8–36; 11:1–40

Persisting in Faith

INTRODUCTION

This week we are going to see the end of one section in Hebrews's argument and the beginning of another. Chapter 10:1–18 finishes up the central argument of Hebrews, which is about how Christ as our High Priest has provided a better sacrifice in a better sanctuary as a better High Priest. These eighteen verses effectively give us the conclusion to that argument. In these verses we see clearly that Christ's death and ascension into heaven have done what the Old Testament sacrificial system could not do. We no longer need to offer animal sacrifices to God.

Hebrews 10:19 then unfolds what this means for the way we live. Mainly, we need to keep going. We need to have faith and be faithful until the end. This is the same message we have already heard over and over in this sermon. Hebrews 11 is, of course, the faith chapter of the Bible. In this chapter, we hear about example after example of individuals who either believed in God when they could not see what he promised or who remained faithful even when life became very difficult. We need to do the same.

ONE

Once and for All

Hebrews 10:8–10, 14 *First he said, "Sacrifices and offerings, burnt offerings and sin offerings you did not desire, nor were you pleased with them"—though they were offered in accordance with the law. ⁹Then he said, "Here I am, I have come to do your will." He sets aside the first to establish the second. ¹⁰And by that* *will, we have been made holy through the sacrifice of the body of Jesus Christ once for all. . . .*

¹⁴*For by one sacrifice he has made perfect forever those who are being made holy.*

Key Observation. We are perfected, cleansed, and made holy in the moment that Christ's sacrifice is applied to us.

Understanding the Word. Hebrews 10:1–18 gives the conclusion to the central argument of Hebrews. As 10:1 begins, Hebrews steps back and looks at the overall significance of what Christ has done in contrast to the Jewish laws about sacrifice. The Law, it concludes, was never actually able to take away sins. Priests of the old covenant offered sacrifices over and over again. If any of them had worked, they could have stopped them.

Instead, Hebrews says, the conscience of those making sacrifices were never cleaned. They kept having to offer more animals. In the end, the Jewish Law only provided a shadowy illustration of the reality that took place in Christ. They were a placeholder, a raincheck. Only with Jesus could that promise of cleansing finally take place.

The author then turned to Psalm 40. The author painted a picture of Christ entering into the world and speaking some of its words. Jesus' entrance into the world was a pronouncement that animal sacrifices and offerings were over. Instead, "a body you prepared for me" (Heb. 10:5). There is a replacement. The body of Jesus would, in fact, take away sins. The body of Jesus would, in fact, cleanse the conscience. The sacrifice of the body of Christ would be a once-and-for-all sacrifice. No sacrifice or offering would ever need to be made again.

As a side note, these words—"a body you prepared for me"—were only in the Greek version the author was using. The Hebrew original read, "my ears you have opened" (Ps. 40:6). It shows that God can speak to us through whatever version of the Bible we are reading.

There is a clear replacement that is taking place here. One system, which was only symbolic in a sense, is being removed. The second is being established. It is ironic in a way that while Hebrews says sins cannot be canceled without the pouring of blood (9:22), not a single instance of that pouring during the old covenant actually worked. Only the death of Christ and his life-giving blood, offered through an eternal Spirit (9:14), could end the need for sacrifice forever.

Christ's one sacrifice has made anyone who comes to him perfect forever. *Perfection* here does not mean moral perfection, although Hebrews clearly expects believers to live in faithfulness. In relation to humanity, *perfection* in Hebrews means our purification and cleansing from sins. When we are perfected by Christ's sacrifice, we are made pure and clean. We are made "holy."

This is a perfection for "those who are being made holy" (10:14) or "those who are being sanctified" (ESV). It would be easy to misread these words. We are so used to the idea of gradual improvement that you might think Hebrews is saying, "every day we are getting a little more holy." But the sense is rather, "Cindy was made holy on Tuesday." "Bob was made holy on Wednesday." "Carla, on Friday." "Those who are being made holy" refers to an ongoing stream of individuals being perfected in a moment, not the course of the life of one individual. In the thinking of Hebrews, we are perfected and made holy in the moment that Christ's sacrifice is applied to us.

1. Being holy means belonging to God and being made pure. Have you ever thought of yourself in that way? How would it change the way you think about yourself if you kept this identity in view?

2. We are not just holy as individuals. We are holy as God's people and God's church. What does it mean for a congregation to be set apart to God? What might it mean for a congregation to be corporately pure?

3. Do these verses give you hope for the world today? Do our attempts to reach God have to end in failure? How can we better trust in the free offering provided through Christ?

TWO

Do It Again

Hebrews 10:32–36 NRSV *But recall those earlier days when, after you had been enlightened, you endured a hard struggle with sufferings,* [33]*sometimes being publicly exposed to abuse and persecution, and sometimes being partners with those so treated.* [34]*For you had compassion for those who were in prison, and you cheerfully accepted the plundering of your possessions, knowing that you yourselves possessed something better and more lasting.* [35]*Do not, therefore, abandon* *that confidence of yours; it brings a great reward.* ³⁶*For you need endurance, so that when you have done the will of God, you may receive what was promised.*

Key Observation. Throughout Hebrews, the author has made it clear that we can count on God to keep his promises. Why would we abandon our hope?

Understanding the Word. In these verses we get another rare glimpse into the past of the congregation to which this sermon was sent. We know from 5:12 and 6:10 that the audience have been believers for some time. Not only have they been believers for a while, but they have endured a previous time of persecution. They had a "hard struggle" during that earlier time. Perhaps some of their leaders lost their lives in that time of persecution (cf. 13:7). They helped some who were in prison. Some of them had their property confiscated.

It is tempting to speculate about these earlier events, even though we do not know for sure where the audience was located. Rome usually receives the most support and, if so, then there are some good candidates for the situation the author had in mind. In the year AD 49, the Roman emperor Claudius expelled all the Jewish Christians from Rome, and some mention that event as possible background for Hebrews. I personally think the persecution of Christians under Nero around the year AD 64 is an even better candidate, since Christians lost their lives in this event.

Some have wondered if Hebrews was written not long after the Romans destroyed Jerusalem and its temple in AD 70. Although it is obvious to us that we do not need a temple because of Christ, we feel this way not least because of Hebrews itself! Before Hebrews, it seems quite possible that some Christians still offered sacrifices in the temple and relied on it for their everyday forgiveness. They may have thought that Jesus took care of the really big forgiveness that Israel and the world needed for ultimate salvation.

If Hebrews was written soon after Jerusalem's destruction, then statements about having no city that remains would make sense (e.g., 13:14). The audience would be demoralized. If they lived in Rome, they would have seen prominent Jews marched through the city and crucified. Such events might definitely have been experienced as God's discipline (cf. 12:7).

Perhaps part of the situation behind Hebrews was the fear that they would have to face that sort of persecution again, although they had not yet shed blood at that time (cf. 12:4). Perhaps they could see the writing on the wall.

Sometimes when we face a certain kind of trial the first time, we do not know what we will have to endure. Ignorance is sometimes a gift from God. But if we face the trial again, the challenge to our willpower may very well be greater.

The author of Hebrews urged the audience to remember the endurance they had once before. He warned them that if they turned away, if they "deliberately keep on sinning" (10:26), there would be no more sacrifice left for them. They have had heaven itself open up to them through Christ (10:20). How horrible it would be indeed, then, to fall into the hands of an angry God (10:31)! Throughout Hebrews, the author has made it clear that we can count on God to keep his promises. Why would we abandon our hope?

1. Have you ever had to face the same kind of trial more than once? Was it easier or harder the second time? How did you rely on God in your time of trial?

2. We do not have to be alone in our struggle against sin. How does facing trials look different when we do it together rather than alone?

3. How does the church engage in mission when it is being persecuted? What is it like to be the church in exile?

THREE

Faith Brings Assurance

Hebrews 11:1–3, 6 ESV *Now faith is the assurance of things hoped for, the conviction of things not seen. ²For by it the people of old received their commendation. ³By faith we understand that the universe was created by the word of God, so that what is seen was not made out of things that are visible. . . .*

⁶And without faith it is impossible to please him, for whoever would draw near to God must believe that he exists and that he rewards those who seek him.

Key Observation. Faith, as it were, is the stuff of what has not happened yet. It gives us now what does not yet exist!

Understanding the Word. Hebrews 10 ends with more encouragement to the audience to persist in their faith, to keep going to the end. As he said back in 6:9, he is confident that the audience will not give up. He is confident they will not abandon the faith or "shrink back" (10:39). He is convinced that they will continue in faith until the day when salvation finally arrives. Using a verse that Paul also used, the audience insisted that "my righteous one will live by faith" and endure to the end.

The Greek word for "faith" had several distinct meanings. It could mean faith in the sense of a trust or a confidence. In other contexts (like James 2), faith could merely refer to a head belief. In other contexts (like Romans 3:3), it could refer to faithfulness.

Hebrews 11 uses the word *faith* both in reference to confidence/trust and in terms of faithfulness. Hebrews 11:1 gives us a good sense of faith as confidence: "faith is the assurance of things hoped for." In terms of human knowledge, we cannot be certain about the things for which we hope. They are still the future so they have not happened yet. We cannot see them.

The King James Version translates this verse to say that faith is the "substance" of things hoped for. Think of it. We do not have the substance yet of what we hope, because it is not here yet. Faith, as it were, is the stuff of what has not happened yet. It gives us now what does not yet exist!

The English Standard Version says that faith is the "conviction" of things not seen. The King James Version says, faith is the "evidence" of things not seen. We cannot see these things with our eyes, but we can see them with the eyes of faith. Faith gives us evidence of what is not evident to human sight.

The universe, Hebrews 11:3 says, was not made out of materials that could be seen. God shaped the universe out of nothing. What faith it would have taken before God created the universe! Yet the fact that God is a God who can make something out of nothing means we can have faith that God will make happen what he has promised.

Hebrews 11:6 then gives a striking statement: if we do not have this sort of confidence, we cannot hope to please God. If we look at the examples of faith in this chapter, faith is not mere belief. It is a conviction that persists for years. In the case of Noah, he had faith for decade upon decade when he could not see any rain. Later in the chapter, the author of Hebrews will talk of people who died with confidence without receiving the promise.

It is thus overwhelmingly clear that Hebrews is talking about a conviction in what God has promised that endures for a lifetime. Without this level of faith, it is impossible to please God. We have to believe that God rewards those who diligently seek him. That is, his promises will come true for those who continue in faith their whole life long. These are those who *diligently* seek him.

1. Are we riding on the fumes of faith past or is our faith up-to-date? Are we pleasing God today?

2. Do you encourage other people around you with your faith? Faith can be as contagious as doubt. Do you add faith to your church?

3. Can you see the evidence of God's hand unseen in the world? Can you see hope in others when no one else can?

FOUR

Our True Homeland

Hebrews 11:13–16 *All these people were still living by faith when they died. They did not receive the things promised; they only saw them and welcomed them from a distance, admitting that they were foreigners and strangers on earth. [14]People who say such things show that they are looking for a country of their own. [15]If they had been thinking of the country they had left, they would have had opportunity to return. [16]Instead, they were longing for a better country—a heavenly one. Therefore God is not ashamed to be called their God, for he has prepared a city for them.*

Key Observation. God's people are always in exile, regardless of appearances, but we also always have hope, because we have the promise of a heavenly city and homeland that is to come.

Understanding the Word. By this point in Hebrews 11, the author has mentioned the faith of Abel, Enoch, Noah, Abraham, Isaac, Jacob, and Sarah. Abel offered the right kind of sacrifice and was killed by someone without faith as a result. By contrast, God rescued Enoch, who was approved because of his faith. Noah built an ark in faith for decades before there was a single drop of rain. He had faith even when there was nothing to see with his eyes.

Abraham left his home to go to a land he had never seen but that God had promised him. Abraham, Isaac, and Jacob all lived in that land that was promised, but it was not theirs while they were there. Sarah and Abraham had faith that God would fulfill the promise of descendants to them even though it did not look possible from a human perspective.

When the author of Hebrews gets to 11:13, he sums up the situation. Abraham, Isaac, and Jacob lived their whole lives and never actually received God's promises, but they still had faith. The implication for the audience is clear. The audience needs to keep going forward with faith and confidence in God's promises whether they see them come to pass or not.

In fact, the author suggests, our entire life here on earth in a sense is a life in a foreign land. We are all immigrants. We are all foreigners and strangers. Our real homeland is in heaven for now. Our true city is nowhere down here on earth at this time. We are looking for it to come. We are expecting God to bring it, but we cannot see it yet.

There is always the danger that these words will lead us to detach. That is not their purpose. The purpose of these words is to encourage the audience of Hebrews in a time of trial and difficulty. Their faith is being challenged by the world they see around them. They need to be reminded that they do not belong to this world. They belong to the next one, a heavenly one.

For many of us the danger is quite the opposite. We are far too comfortable with this world. We have such easy lives that we hardly notice those who are struggling around us. We do not want to see them. We do not want to encounter them. As Paul sarcastically said to the Corinthians, "Already you have all you want! Already you have become rich! You have begun to reign" (1 Cor. 4:8). Perhaps it is more spiritually dangerous for us to have plenty than it is for us to be in need or under persecution!

Hebrews reminds us that we are always exiles on this earth until Christ returns. Indeed, even the visible church is not the true church. Is it possible that even the people of Israel in the Old Testament were never exactly the true Israel? Rather, are God's true people always a subset of those who appear to be God's people? God's true people are those who have faith and who are looking for a heavenly city, whose builder and maker is God (Heb. 11:10).

1. Do you ever feel like you are the only one around with faith? Does it encourage you that we were never truly citizens of this world to begin with?

2. Do you think there are others in the church who are puzzled by your attitudes or actions? Does your life evidence faith? If not, what are you going to do about it?

3. Our faith is a witness to the world, but our faithfulness also judges the world (Heb. 11:7). How serious would you say these truths make our faith?

FIVE

Believing Promises

Hebrews 11:35–40 *Women received back their dead, raised to life again. There were others who were tortured, refusing to be released so that they might gain an even better resurrection. ³⁶Some faced jeers and flogging, and even chains and imprisonment. ³⁷They were put to death by stoning; they were sawed in two; they were killed by the sword. They went about in sheepskins and goatskins, destitute, persecuted and mistreated—³⁸the world was not worthy of them. They wandered in deserts and mountains, living in caves and in holes in the ground.*

³⁹These were all commended for their faith, yet none of them received what had been promised, ⁴⁰since God had planned something better for us so that only together with us would they be made perfect.

Key Observation. The heroes of faith in Hebrews 11 were not able to receive the promise of atonement because only Jesus could bring it. They lived their whole lives with faith without receiving the promise.

Understanding the Word. After the verses from yesterday, Hebrews 11, the faith chapter continues to tell of many other heroes of faith and situations where individuals from Israel's history showed faith of various kinds. Abraham showed faith when he offered Isaac. He knew that Isaac was the child of promise, and yet here was Isaac facing his death. So the audience might face death, but God could bring back the dead.

Jacob and Joseph both saw promises that would come to pass long after their deaths, but they believed them anyway. So the audience of Hebrews needed to believe, whether Jesus saved them or not. Moses' parents faced the threat of the king, but they disobeyed him all the same. So the Roman government might threaten the audience of Hebrews, but they should not fear but move forward in faithfulness.

Moses himself could have enjoyed "the fleeting pleasures of sin" (11:25). He could have enjoyed the opportunities of the world he could see. Instead, he chose to be mistreated as part of the people of God in order that he might receive a great reward later. He could see the invisible God with the eyes of faith, and that faith was the substance of things for which he hoped.

By faith Moses crossed the Red Sea on dry ground. By faith the walls of Jericho fell. Sometimes faith brings victory in this present time and not only in the promised future. By faith Rahab picked the right side, and it was not the side of the people with whom she visibly lived at the time.

It is at this point that we reach the verses above. The author of Hebrews did not tell the individual stories but he listed a number of individuals whose stories of faith could certainly be told. Their stories differ from each other. God granted victory to some over their enemies. Gideon and Barak won. Jephthah and David won. Others did not win. Hebrews 11:35 may refer to a Jewish story about a mother and seven brothers, all of whom had the faith to die in the face of persecution because they believed in the resurrection.

What is very interesting is that Hebrews tells us that none of these actually received the promise in their lifetimes. That is to say, the promise of true cleansing and atonement would have to wait until Jesus Christ. They were not made "perfect" apart from Christ. They died in faith that God would resolve the problem of the world. God would one day solve the problem of the world, but it did not take place while these heroes were alive.

They were waiting for the promise of Christ, a promise that had now come to pass. Now they could be perfected because Christ's offering has been made. Now not only these heroes but the audience of Hebrews could be perfected. Indeed, we can be perfected if we will only continue in faith.

The faith chapter of Hebrews 11 is thus about endurance to the end even more than it is about believing what is not seen. It is about being willing to be sawed in half, as the tradition suggested happened to Isaiah. Sometimes God grants victory over our enemies, but our task is to have faith even if his will is different for us.

1. Are you prepared to live your life out in faith even if it is not God's will to deliver you from trial and persecution?

2. Sometimes we ourselves are not the target of persecution, but we have to decide whether we are going to stand with others who are. Are we prepared to stand with the oppressed, should the time come?

3. There are always Christians-in-waiting watching us on the sidelines. How we react to hard times could be the difference between faith or no faith. Does that create any resolve in you?

WEEK SEVEN

GATHERING DISCUSSION OUTLINE

A. Open session in prayer.

B. View video for this week's readings.

C. What general impressions and thoughts do you have after considering the video and reading the daily writings on these Scriptures? How have you grown deeper in your faith and understanding of Scripture?

D. Discuss questions selected from the daily readings.

    1. **KEY OBSERVATION:** We are perfected, cleansed, and made holy in the moment that Christ's sacrifice is applied to us.

    DISCUSSION QUESTION: We are not just holy as individuals. We are holy as God's people and God's church. What does it mean for a congregation to be set apart to God? What might it mean for a congregation to be corporately pure?

    2. **KEY OBSERVATION:** Throughout Hebrews, the author has made it clear that we can count on God to keep his promises. Why would we abandon our hope?

    DISCUSSION QUESTION: How does the church engage in mission when it is being persecuted? What is it like to be the church in exile?

    3. **KEY OBSERVATION:** Faith, as it were, is the stuff of what has not happened yet. It gives us now what does not yet exist!

DISCUSSION QUESTION: Can you see the evidence of God's hand unseen in the world? Can you see hope in others when no one else can?

4. **KEY OBSERVATION:** God's people are always in exile, regardless of appearances, but we also always have hope, because we have the promise of a heavenly city and homeland that is to come.

   DISCUSSION QUESTION: Do you think there are others in the church who are puzzled by your attitudes or actions? Does your life evidence faith? If not, what are you going to do about it?

5. **KEY OBSERVATION:** The heroes of faith in Hebrews 11 were not able to receive the promise of atonement because only Jesus could bring it. They lived their whole lives with faith without receiving the promise.

   DISCUSSION QUESTION: Are you prepared to live your life out in faith even if it is not God's will to deliver you from trial and persecution?

E. Close session with prayer.

WEEK EIGHT

Hebrews 12:1–24; 13:1–10

The Heavenly Jerusalem

INTRODUCTION

This week we finish the book of Hebrews by walking through Hebrews 12 and 13. After the author has been encouraging the audience to continue in faith for a chapter and a half, he then reflects about how the Lord disciplines his children. Discipline is not particularly pleasant, but it helps us grow and keeps us on the right track. Chapter 12 ends with both a beautiful picture of heaven and also a fearful picture of judgment.

Hebrews 13 then seems to shift from sermon to letter conclusion. This chapter ends Hebrews with the kind of instruction that Paul might put at the end of one of his letters. There is some miscellaneous encouragement to live the right way and some curious instruction to stay away from a certain strange teaching.

There are some intriguing hints about the situation behind Hebrews at the end. Timothy is mentioned, Paul's missionary partner. He has been in jail for his faith—could it be in Ephesus? Greetings are sent from some Italians, possibly indicating that Hebrews was intended for a congregation in Rome.

ONE

A Cloud of Witnesses

Hebrews 12:1–3 NRSV *Therefore, since we are surrounded by so great a cloud of witnesses, let us also lay aside every weight and the sin that clings so closely, and let us run with perseverance the race that is set before us, [2]looking to Jesus the pioneer and perfecter of our faith, who for the sake of the joy that was set before* *him endured the cross, disregarding its shame, and has taken his seat at the right hand of the throne of God.*

³Consider him who endured such hostility against himself from sinners, so that you may not grow weary or lose heart.

Key Observation. The race of faith is the race of a lifetime. We do not know how long we will be running nor do we know the precise course ahead.

Understanding the Word. These verses give us the takeaway from Hebrews 11. The faith chapter has given us numerous examples of faith. These are individuals who acted on a reality that they could not yet see. They continued on a course believing that it led to the place God had told them it led. They endured suffering and persecution because they had faith that God was real and would come through in the end. Sometimes they died in this life, trusting in the world to come.

Hebrews 12 then seems to give us the image of a stadium where we are running. In the stands are all these heroes of faith from the Old Testament. They ran this race once. They finished it. Now they are cheering us on as we run. Their lives are an encouragement for us to finish the race too.

If you are a runner, you know that there are short races and there are long races. You do not run a long race the way you run a short one. In the 100-meter dash, you run as fast as you can the entire race. It is an all-out sprint!

But the 1600-meter race in track is quite different, and the five-kilometer race in cross-country is different too. A marathon is more than twenty-six miles. It requires a lot of training to finish, even if you are a natural runner.

The race of faith is a long-distance run. It is the race of life. It is a race that we have to run with great patience, because it takes a lifetime to finish and the results last for eternity. We do not know how long we will be running nor do we know the course ahead. It is a race of faith.

The faith we have had in the past is our training for the faith we will need in the future. You cannot simply run a marathon if you have not been training. In the same way, we probably will not fare well in the testing of our faith if we have not been exercising our faith up to this point. Is it possible that some of the doubt that people have in times of testing is at times a reflection of what they have been doing with their faith before the trial came?

Hebrews 12 encourages us to look to Jesus as we run. Although we do not always think of Jesus as an example for us, Hebrews certainly does. Jesus ran this race too. Jesus, in fact, was the first to run the Christian race. He made the race possible in the first place. He saw what the finish line looked like. He knew it was a "joy" that was set before him.

Jesus endured the cross. He rejected the shame associated with this cruel instrument of the Romans. Individuals were crucified naked, to bring the maximum disgrace and humiliation. But Jesus "despised" all that. He was willing to endure such hostility because he saw the end game and had faith.

Hebrews encouraged its audience—and us—to have faith as well. We need to lay aside any extra weight. You do not normally run in jeans or in a coat. If you are a serious runner, you buy lightweight shoes. Sin—especially a lack of faith—will only hinder our running. Hebrews says to take it off.

1. Is there any weight of sin that is hindering you from running the race of faith? Why not take off that weight today?

2. Do you cheer others on in their race of faith? How can you come alongside them and offer them a cool drink of water, or even run with them for a stint?

3. Our running can inspire others to run as well. Have you invited anyone to run with you lately?

TWO

Endure the Training

Hebrews 12:7–10 *Endure hardship as discipline; God is treating you as his children. For what children are not disciplined by their father? ⁸If you are not disciplined—and everyone undergoes discipline—then you are not legitimate, not true sons and daughters at all. ⁹Moreover, we have all had human fathers who disciplined us and we respected them for it. How much more should we submit to the Father of spirits and live! ¹⁰They disciplined us for a little while as they thought best; but God disciplines us for our good, in order that we may share in his holiness.*

Key Observation. While God's discipline does not seem pleasant at the time, God uses it to get us back on course and to strengthen us for the time of trial.

Understanding the Word. After the beginning of Hebrews 12 encouraged the audience to keep running, we get the smallest of hints about their situation in 12:4. In their struggle against sin, they have not yet lost blood. That is to say, the audience is presumably facing the possibility of persecution. They have suffered before, and perhaps they can see the cloud of suffering rising on the horizon. Perhaps they are already feeling the pressure.

This encouragement reminds the author of Proverbs 3:11–12, where the discipline of the Lord is compared to the discipline a parent might give to a child. Both Proverbs and Hebrews give us a very positive view of discipline. Often, when we hear the word *discipline*, we think about punishment. A child does wrong and the parent punishes them to satisfy some sense of justice.

But this is not the sense of discipline in Hebrews 12. It is true that there is a hint of discipline as correction in this chapter. Discipline in this sense is about correcting the child's path or direction. Notice how constructive discipline is in this case. It is not administered because of some abstract sense of justice but for the good of the child!

This is an important fact to keep in mind. When we discipline our children or anyone under our supervision or authority, our goal should not principally be justice. The goal is not to satisfy some abstract law of the universe. In our interpersonal relationships, the purpose of discipline is correction and redirection. We want the person under discipline to get better, not only for the sake of ourselves and others but for their own sake.

There is also another sense to the word *discipline* lurking about in this passage. The word for discipline also means training. If you are going to run a race, you need to have discipline and train. The audience of Hebrews and, indeed, all of us are in training. We need to learn discipline so that when trials come, we will be ready.

Hebrews tells this congregation that they are undergoing the Lord's discipline, like a father might discipline a son. Parents, we know, are not always consistent in such discipline. At times they get it wrong. But God's discipline always gets it right. He is the Father of our spirits and he is training our souls for spiritual battle.

The end result of such training is that we share in God's holiness. The author of Hebrews hints that there are some parents who punish inconsistently and according to their whim or how they are feeling at the moment. God does not discipline in that way. God disciplines us for our good.

To share in God's holiness is for Hebrews, at the very least, to be cleansed of all sin. As verse 11 goes on to say, "No discipline seems pleasant at the time, but painful. Later on, however, it produces a harvest of righteousness and peace for those who have been trained by it." So God's discipline makes us live more righteously and results in peace with God.

1. Have you ever undergone a time of redirection that you might identify as God's discipline? What good did it bring in your spiritual life?

2. Have you ever seen God discipline a community? What might that look like?

3. Not all trials are the discipline of God. Sometimes others cause hardship of their free will. Sometimes God does not command but allows bad things to happen. How would you tell the difference?

THREE

The Heavenly Celebration

Hebrews 12:22–24 ESV *But you have come to Mount Zion and to the city of the living God, the heavenly Jerusalem, and to innumerable angels in festal gathering, [23]and to the assembly of the firstborn who are enrolled in heaven, and to God, the judge of all, and to the spirits of the righteous made perfect, [24]and to Jesus, the mediator of a new covenant, and to the sprinkled blood that speaks a better word than the blood of Abel.*

Key Observation. Those who have gone before us are already in heaven in festive assembly. They are worshipping God and the Lamb with their sins forgiven.

Understanding the Word. The verses between yesterday's passage and today's include some stern warnings to the congregation. In 12:12–13, the author quoted Proverbs again with some instruction telling them, in effect, to stop slouching and pull themselves together. We have yet another stern warning to the congregation, in some ways the most startling of all.

Hebrews suggests that bitterness can take root in a person and not only make you impure but can "defile" many around you as well. The example he raised is that of Esau. Esau was the firstborn, and so had what they called the "birthright." The firstborn son in those days inherited all or mostly all of his father's possessions. But Esau's younger brother, Jacob, was crafty and caught Esau in a moment of weakness, when he was returning from days of unsuccessful hunting. Esau sold Jacob his birthright for some food.

The most startling statement Hebrews makes comes in 12:17, which says that Esau could not find a place of repentance, even though he sought it eagerly with tears. Hebrews seems to say that there is a point where the audience could go so far away from Christ in turning their backs on him, that they might not be able to find the heart to repent. Perhaps they might know with their head that they need to repent, but they just might not be able to do so any more.

Here we are reminded that the Holy Spirit is what empowers our ability to repent. Christians do not believe that we have the power in ourselves to come to God. It is only by God's grace and power that we can find a place of true turning and repentance. These truths raise the scary possibility that those who have said no to God their entire lives may not find themselves able to come to God at the end, even if they know with their heads that they need to. A heart of stone can only become a heart of flesh by a miracle of God. Thankfully, anyone who still feels the tug of God on their heart has not reached this point!

The verses for today paint a much better picture. The audience has not come to Mount Sinai as in the Old Testament (12:18–21). They have not become part of the old covenant with Moses. They have come to the heavenly Jerusalem and the true Mount Zion. This is the city prepared for them that the author mentioned in 11:16.

In that heavenly city are tens of thousands of angels in festive assembly. Jesus is there, the One who has brokered the new covenant. There are the spirits of countless righteous individuals there as well.

This is both a picture of this present time and a picture of what is to come. Those who have gone before us are already in heaven worshipping God and the Lamb. If we die before Christ returns, there will come a time when we will join that festive, heavenly assembly.

There will also come a day when Christ will return to earth. Then every knee will bow and tongue confess that Jesus, the Messiah, is Lord! God will shake the heavens and the earth (12:26), and we as Christians believe God will establish a new heaven and a new earth.

1. Have you ever considered the possibility that someone's heart could become so hardened, even if they had once been a believer, that they could never find a place of repentance?

2. Have you ever thought of our worship here on earth as a participation in the worship that is going on constantly in heaven? How might that affect the way you worship in church?

3. The end of Hebrews 12 speaks of the shaking of the heavens and earth in their current form. Why would we not do everything we can to make sure as many people as possible do not experience that event?

FOUR

Live On

Hebrews 13:1–5 NRSV *Let mutual love continue. ²Do not neglect to show hospitality to strangers, for by doing that some have entertained angels without knowing it. ³Remember those who are in prison, as though you were in prison with them; those who are being tortured, as though you yourselves were being tortured. ⁴Let marriage be held in honor by all, and let the marriage bed be kept undefiled; for God will judge fornicators and adulterers. ⁵Keep your lives free from the love of money, and be content with what you have; for he has said, "I will never leave you or forsake you."*

Key Observation. The promise that God will not leave us or forsake us remains true for all time. Even when it may not look like God is around, he is lovingly watching over us.

Understanding the Word. The sermon part of Hebrews ends with chapter 12. Hebrews 13 then looks a lot like the conclusion to a letter. Although most scholars do not think Paul was the author of Hebrews, chapter 13 does look similar to the conclusions of some of Paul's letters. Timothy is even mentioned in 13:23. So it seems likely that the author of Hebrews was someone close to Paul's circle, although we will never know exactly who.

Hebrews 13 begins with miscellaneous instruction that would be appropriate for any church even today: "Let mutual love continue." Christians need to love each other.

The instruction to show hospitality to others may seem somewhat strange to us. We live in an age of hotels and easy travel. In the ancient world, showing kindness to traveling visitors was a significant virtue. In fact, in Matthew 10:15, Jesus seems to be saying that failure to welcome the angels was one of the primary sins of Sodom and Gomorrah.

The idea that angels might be among us disguised as strangers is not a typical one for us. But it highlights the biblical value of helping the stranger, the foreigner, the alien. You may have heard stories of helpers who seem to appear out of nowhere to help in times of need. So we are called to treat those we do not know who are "not from around here" with loving-kindness.

Marriage is always under the threat of lust and unfaithfulness. The prevalence of divorce today is not because the human heart has become more lustful. We are only now freer to play it out legally. Most divorce though is probably the result of bitterness that accumulates because we cannot forgive each other. Despite these challenges, marriage remains God's desire, a treasure to be protected.

The love of money remains as much a danger as ever. Indeed, because the Western world has made prosperity so attainable, the dangers of being too comfortable are more threatening than before. We have more, but we are less content than ever. We either hoard it when we could help others in need or we squander it on ourselves. This is not the biblical way!

The mention of prisoners reminds us that Hebrews was written at a tough time for many Christians. At the time this sermon was written, there were Christians around the world who were in jail awaiting a verdict. Prison was not a final punishment in the Roman Empire, but more where a person awaited sentencing. Once sentenced, the judgment was administered immediately.

If you did not have help on the outside, there was no cafeteria inside. Prisoners like Paul relied on the support of other Christians to live. And the Roman legal system was not fast.

The promise that God will not leave us or forsake us remains true for all time. Even when it may not look like God is around, he is lovingly watching over us. He is protecting us when we do not know it. He is guiding us when we feel unsure of our direction. If he allows us to suffer, he does so painfully because of some bigger picture that we usually cannot see.

1. How do you as an individual measure up against the virtues that Hebrews calls on its audience to follow? Go down the list.

2. It is so easy for us to get preoccupied with our own concerns that we miss the importance of brotherly love and helping one another. Have you kept others in sight as you go about your life?

3. Who are some strangers that we as individuals, as the church, and as a society might be hospitable to, even if they are not believers? What would a thoroughgoing hospitality look like?

FIVE

We Have an Altar

Hebrews 13:7–10 *Remember your leaders, who spoke the word of God to you. Consider the outcome of their way of life and imitate their faith. [8]Jesus Christ is the same yesterday and today and forever.*

[9]Do not be carried away by all kinds of strange teachings. It is good for our hearts to be strengthened by grace, not by eating ceremonial foods, which is of no benefit to those who do so. [10]We have an altar from which those who minister at the tabernacle have no right to eat.

Key Observation. Hebrews assures us that God is still God, Jesus' sacrifice still atones for all sin, and the promises for which we hope are all still true.

Understanding the Word. The last part of Hebrews 13 continues to give closing instructions to this community and wishes God's blessing on them. The author of Hebrews prays a blessing over them, praying that God will equip them fully in order to do his will. He remembers as he blesses them that the God to which they are praying brought Jesus up from the dead. He speaks of

Jesus as the Great Shepherd of the sheep, making us think of the characteristics of a shepherd in Psalm 23.

In these last verses, Hebrews twice mentions leaders of the church, past and present. Of the present leaders, Hebrews instructs the congregation or congregations to submit to the authority of their current leaders and have confidence in them. The role of such leaders is clear—they are to watch over the audience. They are there to help the church stay on course and not go astray. This task can be a joyful one or it can be a very difficult one.

The same goes for us today. Do we make it easy for our church leaders to keep the church on track, or are we a constant source of difficulty? Leaders, of course, are neither perfect nor always correct. Sometimes they can make our Christian walk less joyous and more difficult. But whoever we are and whatever role we play, we can be a source of joy more than a source of difficulty.

Hebrews also remembers some leaders from the past. When it mentions the "outcome" of their lives, we wonder if they were put to death for their faith. If Hebrews was written to Rome, we can easily imagine that people like the apostle Paul and the apostle Peter were in mind. They were put to death by the Roman emperor Nero at some point in the 60s.

When the author pointed out that Jesus "is the same yesterday and today and forever," he was indicating that just as Jesus was faithful to their leaders during suffering in the past, he will be faithful to them in their present and, indeed, he will be faithful to us today whatever we may face in our lives. The character of Jesus is constant, and the author reminded us of it several times. He is a Priest who wants to help us and who sympathizes with us. He is our Brother. He is our Shepherd. He was the pioneer of the race that is set before us, and he is waiting for us at the finish line.

In these final verses, Hebrews also hints of something that might tempt the audience—"strange teaching." There is some "food" that connected to the earthly sacrificial system. The author reminds them of the central argument of the sermon. We have all the food we need in Jesus' atoning sacrifice. They need not worry about some connection to the temple (if it was still standing) or to the synagogue (if it was thought to substitute now in some way for the temple). Jesus took care of it all!

The book of Hebrews was a word of exhortation to a congregation struggling to keep going. They were facing persecution and possibly events that seemed puzzling in the light of God's promises. The author assured them that

God is still God, that Jesus' atonement stands forever, and that the promises for which they hope are still true.

1. Is there anything in your life that you are tempted to substitute for the genuine food from God?

2. We eat from God's table together as a community. Does your community of faith all eat the one bread and drink the one cup of Jesus Christ?

3. Does your community respect its leaders? Is it a joy for your leaders to shepherd the flock or a constant struggle?

WEEK EIGHT

GATHERING DISCUSSION OUTLINE

A. Open session in prayer.

B. View video for this week's readings.

C. What general impressions and thoughts do you have after considering the video and reading the daily writings on these Scriptures? How have you grown deeper in your faith and understanding of Scripture?

D. Discuss questions selected from the daily readings.

    1. **KEY OBSERVATION:** The race of faith is the race of a lifetime. We do not know how long we will be running nor do we know the precise course ahead.

    DISCUSSION QUESTION: Is there any weight of sin that is hindering you from running the race of faith? Why not take off that weight today?

    2. **KEY OBSERVATION:** While God's discipline does not seem pleasant at the time, God uses it to get us back on course and to strengthen us for the time of trial.

    DISCUSSION QUESTION: Not all trials are the discipline of God. Sometimes others cause hardship of their free will. Sometimes God does not command but allows bad things to happen. How would you tell the difference?

3. **KEY OBSERVATION:** Those who have gone before us are already in heaven in festive assembly. They are worshipping God and the Lamb with their sins forgiven.

   DISCUSSION QUESTION: Have you ever thought of our worship here on earth as a participation in the worship that is going on constantly in heaven? How might that affect the way you worship in church?

4. **KEY OBSERVATION:** The promise that God will not leave us or forsake us remains true for all time. Even when it may not look like God is around, he is lovingly watching over us.

   DISCUSSION QUESTION: Who are some strangers that we as individuals, as the church, and as a society might be hospitable to, even if they are not believers? What would a thoroughgoing hospitality look like?

5. **KEY OBSERVATION:** Hebrews assures us that God is still God, Jesus' sacrifice still atones for all sin, and the promises for which we hope are all still true.

   DISCUSSION QUESTION: We eat from God's table together as a community. Does your community of faith all eat the one bread and drink the one cup of Jesus Christ?

E. Close session with prayer.

FOR FURTHER STUDY

Cockerill, Gareth. *Hebrews: A Bible Commentary in the Wesleyan Tradition.* Indianapolis: Wesleyan Publishing, 1999.

deSilva, David A. *Perseverance in Gratitude: A Socio-Rhetorical Commentary on the Epistle to the Hebrews.* Grand Rapids: Eerdmans, 2000.

Guthrie, George. *Hebrews: The NIV Application Commentary.* Grand Rapids: Zondervan, 1998.

Hagner, Donald. *Encountering the Book of Hebrews.* Grand Rapids: Baker Academic, 2002.

Johnson, Luke Timothy. *Hebrews.* Louisville: Westminster John Knox, 2006.

Schenck, Kenneth. *Understanding the Book of Hebrews: The Story Behind the Sermon.* Louisville: Westminster John Knox, 2003.

Wright, N. T. *Hebrews for Everyone.* Louisville: Westminster John Knox, 2003.

why is the promised so important

Jews believe that start of the relationships beteen God and the Jews People

Mount Zion) is where Yahweh , the God of Isreal dwells , King david & Jesus

9 781628 245202